PRAYING THE WORD OF GRACE

THE REVIVAL OF A GRIEVING FATHER'S SOUL THROUGH THE SIMPLE PRACTICE OF SCRIPTURE-BASED PRAYER

JONAH PRIOUR

LOVEBUILT PRESS

Scripture Quotations:

All Scripture quotations are from Bible translations that are either in the public domain, or have been used by permission. A "Translation Index" has been included at the end of this book, with copyright information from every translation used.

ISBN:

978-1-963124-00-2 (Ebook)

978-1-963124-01-9 (Paperback)

978-1-963124-02-6 (Hardcover)

LCCN:

Library of Congress Control Number: 2024906951

To my beautiful wife, Faith. My "fellow heir of the grace of life," my gift from above, priceless crown of grace. Thank you for all you are.

To my parents. You raised me in God's love. You are living examples of what it means to follow when we are "called by His grace."

To my dear friend, D. W. Martin. Brother in Christ and mentor in the gospel of grace. You taught me to "take hold of that for which Christ Jesus took hold of me."

At last, to our Judah. You will always be "our little hero".

And now I entrust you to God and to the word of His grace ...

— ACTS 20:32 (NASB)

CONTENTS

INTRODUCTION

INTO THE ARMS OF GRACE

I suppose this book has been inside me for a long time. And yet ... I didn't sit down to write all of it at first.

Originally, I set out to make a simple collection of scriptures on the theme of grace, and crafted declarations to go with them. I've been wanting to have that kind of book in my hands for years.

As I dug more into the idea, however, all of these deep memories began to surface.

Times when God came to my rescue with His Word, piercing through my thick darkness with His glorious light.

Or these times of rich, intimate encounter with the Holy Spirit, that I experienced when I would pray the words of Scripture.

I don't know where I'd be without God and His grace ...

Exploring the theme of grace was opening some deep places in my soul and letting the light in on some rooms I'd not originally intended to open up in this book. As the memories flooded in, an overflow of gratitude and passion welled up inside me and compelled me to write more. I found myself immersed.

It began to seem as though two books were forming ... or maybe two parts of the same book.

I just want to share an honest moment with you. While I have been so deeply moved by the process of writing out these very personal stories, the idea of releasing them hasn't been an easy one. I'm not even sure why. Maybe it's just the vulnerability of sharing all of this openly. Did I really want to share all this now? Do I honestly feel ready?

Maybe it's the voices of inadequacy that I'm sure many writers face. The anxiousness that an idea has not been developed enough, *or too much*, followed by the compulsion to tweak this or that just a few more times ... or a few hundred more times. Gulp. I know, I know ... Years from now, these worries will probably all appear quite silly in the grand scheme of things. But for the moment, my stomach has been in knots!

Oh well. Welcome to my thought process. I suppose even the writing of this book has been an exercise in leaning into God's amazing grace.

Well, I also wondered, what if it was God bringing those memories and imagery to mind, to illustrate the message of grace found in the scriptures and prayers of the second part? Maybe the book needed them. That's the feedback I got as I read pieces to others, to "please keep" the stories and other stuff in there.

I took a deep breath. Truthfully, my story belongs to God anyway. It's His story. What good thing do I have that I haven't freely received? And what else is there to do, except freely give it away? He is so worthy of that. He has been so faithful.

It really is my deepest honor to share with you how my life has been transformed by God and the word of His grace. That's the very best thing I could give.

My greatest desire and prayer for this book is for anyone who reads this to meet God and His grace, however that may look. And if anything in my story can help one person in theirs, then it's all worth it to me.

Besides, His grace is sufficient, and made perfect through human weakness, right? I know I'll make my mistakes in the process and improve in the next work. But that's just life. There's no other journey than the one we're on.

And I suppose, I'm exactly the kind of guy God's grace shines through. You know, the human kind. This is *precisely* where grace happens. God is the perfection. He's the star of the show. And He is the light I pray you see. *And oh, what a glorious Light ...*

Still, those anxious thoughts can be persistent little things ... They'd come on strong in the middle of a restless night, and start searching for a way out of this, inventing clever reasons to shelve the more personal stuff for "some day in the future" and just go back to the prayers and scriptures where it all started. After all, this is my first book ever, I'd be more prepared later, et cetera ...

Well, God is even more clever ... and He gives more grace. And, as it turns out, my wife Faith is more persistent, and has a strong gift of encouragement. She asked for only one thing this Christmas: that I publish my book, with all of it included.

Checkmate. I am actually laughing as I type this. Okay God, You got me. And I swear, over the last month I've had dozens of confirmations that this is the way forward. His grace kept finding me. He'd speak through people, scriptures, random events ... not so random events ...

I came to see, yet again, this has always been the story. Moses. Gideon. The apostles. Hasn't this same conversation with God happened throughout history?

"Who, me?" ... *"Yes, you."*

"But what about my weakness?" ... *"But what about My grace?"*

Well. If all of this was just so God could show me something wonderful about His grace ... It has certainly worked. And, for that alone, it would have been *so worth it*. But, I have a feeling He has a whole lot of glorious grace to show other people through this, too.

And honestly, at this point I'm just so grateful. Thank You, God, for your faithful and determined love, and for Your amazing and limitless grace upon grace.

Sometimes, the best way out is through.

Well, Faithie, what can I say? Tis the season!

This one's for you. *Here I go.*

This book is written in two parts.

The original idea has now become Part Two. This part includes 31 chapters of curated scriptures, gathered around the theme of grace. Each chapter is concluded by in-depth prayers crafted from its list of scriptures: filled with declarations of who God is, who we are in Christ, and what we have been given by His grace.

Each scripture is repeated from several different translations, to observe it from different angles. Keep that in mind when looking at the page count!

Truly, this second part can stand on its own. And you can skip right to it, if you'd like.

But, as I've explained, there is now also a Part One. This part includes a few of my own personal stories of experiencing God when I needed Him most, with a focus on meeting God through Scripture.

I have received great grace in times of great need. I pray that in sharing a few of these moments, they will become meeting places for you and the Father of all comfort, where He can give you the same in your life.

This first part also includes some background and imagery that has really inspired me, and deeply enriched my prayer life. These ideas are meant to set a context for our reading, empower us with tools, and invigorate the purpose of the second part. So we can "jump in" more wholeheartedly into the ocean of grace.

I've called these two parts "Part One: Preparing the Table" (some of the stories, scriptures, images and ideas that led up to this book) and "Part Two: Enjoying the Feast" (praying through the glorious word of grace).

God "prepares a feast" for us (Psalm 23:5, NLT) and invites us to "share a meal together as friends" (Revelation 3:20, NLT). Our Father is the kind who welcomes His children with open arms, celebrates them, and throws feasts for them with music and dancing (Luke 15:22-24).

There are many ways we could frame the journey ahead. Something about the image of the feast just captivates me as I write this. It speaks of God's abundance, the generosity and love flowing from the Father's heart, and the nourishing life found in His word of grace. It makes me think of the wonderful fellowship we have with God. It reminds me of family. It reminds me of grace.

This book is written with so many sincere prayers behind it, from many people, that it would be an open door for you to encounter God and His grace, and come to know them more (2 Peter 3:18, John 17:3). I pray that through it, God sets the table of grace for you, and with Him, you feast on His glorious words (Jeremiah 15:16, Psalm 119:103).

Lastly, I don't know where you're at as you pick up this book.

Maybe you are simply excited to enrich your communion with God. And I pray you'll find just that. *Abundantly so!*

Maybe you have felt despair or devastation, and need hope again. I know that feeling. I know what it's like to feel alone and to feel like I no longer found the life force to get up off the ground.

I also know what it's like to be held by the grace of God, and hear the truth whispered in my ear, that I was never alone. To be saved by grace, strengthened by grace, to see God break through and revive me with His grace, and to be inspired once again by His amazing, unending grace ...

Man. The God of grace really has met me time and time again, reaching into my life through so many creative and wonderful avenues. And often, this came through the simple, yet powerful tool of praying God's Word. And that's what this book is all about.

I suppose this is also a book about letting go and falling into the arms of grace, which is an act of faith in itself. And in those loving, capable arms, rests the life we were truly made for all along.

So, maybe in this spirit of trust, we can fall into His arms together. Let's draw courage from the eyes of Jesus, and power from His Word, to reach out and take hold of all that God has for us.

You know, I'm really getting excited now. I think it's all going to be worth it. We were made for this! So what are we waiting for? It's time to take the leap.

Are you ready? *Here we go.*

Merry Christmas, Faith!

PART I

PREPARING THE TABLE

Psalm 23:5

"You prepare a table before me ..." (NKJV)
"You prepare a feast for me ..." (NLT)

Jeremiah 15:16

"When your words turned up, I feasted on them; and they became my joy, the delight of my heart, because I belong to you ..." (CEB)

1 John 1:1

"That which was from the beginning, which we have heard, which we have seen with our own eyes, which we have gazed upon and touched with our own hands — this is the Word of life." (BSB)

∼

My story of how this book came to be.
May the Word meet you here.

1

A LIGHT SHINES IN THE DARKNESS

Your word is a lamp to my feet and a light to my path. *(Psalm 119:105, ESV)*

I am so thankful for the Scripture.

So is my wife, Faith.

If you were to ask her about this, she'd probably crack a smile and tell you about this collection of laminated papers that I've pinned up in the showers of various houses we've lived in through the years. The pages are packed full of verses on both sides, single space, narrow margins. All on some theme. Faith, rest, prayers & benedictions, that kind of thing.

Being the one of us with far better style, she might chuckle at how the shower wall looked a bit cluttered, but might also concede to the payoff of reciting the verses as we washed off the dust of the day.

She might tell you about the assortment of narrators' voices we've heard through the years, reading the Word of God on audio, filling up the different rooms in our houses ... and filling our cars ... and our headphones as we jogged around the block.

Or she'd possibly tell you about these precious "Scripture Lullabies" we found one year, and would play and sing for our children. Or maybe about the Bibles, verse memory cards, and promise books scattered around coffee tables, on bookshelves, and on our nightstands, right beside where our heads hit the pillow each night. She might mention a lot of things, if you were to ask her.

I know one thing ...

She would tell you about 2017.

July 13, 2017 began the most beautiful and miraculous ... and the most terrifying, darkest season of our lives.

It was the night our firstborn son, Judah, was born.

Earlier in the afternoon, we had gone to our regular appointment with a perinatal specialist. I learned a lot of words on this journey I didn't know about before. That's the doctor you see when your pregnancy is flagged as "high-risk".

Well, Judah got the flag. Partly because of the three miscarriages my Faith had before this pregnancy, each one very rare in its diagnosis. Also partly because of the inconclusive yet concerning "signs" that had been showing up in scans the more this pregnancy progressed.

We had been praying constantly through a lot of things, as the doctors kept a close eye. We resolved to encourage ourselves in the Lord, saying that no flag or label could truly identify our son, or Faith or me, except for what God said about us. We still believe that.

That day, the specialist saw something concerning in Judah's heartbeat:

"I don't like that at all. We need to get you in. As in, right now."

We weren't expecting this. Even though we knew there would be some element of surprise in any birthing experience, we didn't think it would be in this way.

Well, I guess this is it. We're having a baby.

We packed up quickly, and went to the hospital for Faith to have an emergency c-section. All the while, continuing to pray. We went into that procedure holding our breath, with no idea of what to expect. Just trusting God and holding on tight.

Everything happened very quickly that night. So, hold on tight with us ...

As I walked in, the room felt loaded with urgency. It was in the voices of all the team. My wife was strapped down, surrendered in love to a process that no doubt felt incredibly scary. I sat by her head, and we held each other, praying and singing worship songs. From that moment forth, the stakes felt constantly high.

Judah Michael was born on July 13, 2017, at 6:04 PM, weighing 3 lbs. 12 oz.

And his little body was in extremely critical condition.

Our early moments with our newborn son in that room were brief. We caught glimpses of his face, and then watched him get rushed away in a flash to the NICU for urgent care.

Love and fear seemed to both hang thickly in the air, like a buildup of two intense, opposing forces fighting for space.

I'll never forget the fear and love that I felt, and so much else … seeing my son's eyes for the first time. And I'll never forget the harrowing look I saw on his face.

A look of utter survival. A look that cried:

help.

I followed the team into the NICU as fast as I could get there. I got to Judah's bedside, and felt the compelling feeling I'd become very acquainted with: of wanting so badly to do anything to help, yet not knowing exactly what to do.

So I sat down in the corner and prayed fervently under my breath while the team was at work. This is what I would do. This was my battle station for the moment.

I sat there in a mix of shell shock and determined love as I watched them set up my firstborn son in his first crib: a hospital incubator. Tubes and wires were being attached to him from every direction while they tried to move air through his lungs with a bag, literally breathing his breaths for him.

My focus was absolutely immersed. All the while, tempestuous waves seemed to keep crashing in from every direction. I was trying to be fully present, and still communicate with my wife everything I could while they had her in recovery. Not to mention a team of family and friends, waiting on the edge of their seats, praying with us.

We would come to find out later that Judah was born with a disorder that basically sent distorted messages to his whole body during its formation. His heart. His lungs. His liver. His joints. *Everything was struggling.*

Specialist after specialist visited to tell us more news. They drew diagrams of all the things going wrong inside our little boy. Critical decisions were being made. We were told in somber tones what this might mean for the days ahead. And our heads were spinning.

Somehow, though, God still felt so present in the middle of all this. Somehow, He brought peace, clarity, and courage to our hearts and minds.

I'm telling you, a level of resolve took over us that could only be explained by the presence of God, holding us together by the second, sustaining and empowering us supernaturally. We were absolutely determined to fight for Judah, and give every ounce of love we had to that little boy.

And when we felt we had no life left in us, God would show up with more. And more. And more.

Again. And again ... *and again.*

Oh God ... how could I ever describe it ...

I would tell you that it was messy at times, but that doesn't really even come close to describing the journey. The only words I can find at the moment are:

I don't know where we'd be without the grace of God.

Well, it may seem odd to jump out of the story here, with only a few snapshots in hand. But friend, Judah's story is an entire book of its own. Actually, I imagine his life may well inspire many books. Those will come someday.

For now, I will tell you this ... Judah will always be our little hero. He has touched countless lives, and continues to. We miss him more than words can say, and we are so, so proud of him ...

And God is ever the Champion of this story. I believe Life will get the last word ... I believe that Love ultimately won the fight for the territory of our hearts, and our history ...

So, how did we get here, in a book about praying the Scripture?

Well, I told you how grateful we are for God's written Word. To share our hearts with you on this, means to share our Judah with you.

Because during that time of great darkness, the Word of God became the lamp to our feet. Like a beacon of hope emerging in the night, it came to our rescue to light the way.

The same promises of God, which we had recited in the shower, began to come to our remembrance in the chaos at the NICU. They would rise up within us, and with them, we began to speak peace to the storms around us, as well as the storms within us.

They were there at just the right time, right when we needed them most.

We got thrown into an unexpected fight. And, thank God, He had a storehouse of weapons, that were not of this world. These weapons were mighty in God, and had divine power to demolish arguments that would rise up against the knowledge of God, and bring them under the obedience of Christ (2 Corinthians 10:4-6).

The Word of God is called the "sword of the spirit" (Ephesians 6:17). And as we held it in our hands, we saw it had real power to fight against the "raging thoughts" and "opposing imaginations." And there were definitely plenty of those.

But our God is greater.

And what a little warrior our Judah was.

And let me tell you, he was surrounded by fellow soldiers.

I don't know how to explain it. These memories are filled with such a powerful sense of connection, purpose, presence ... Maybe we could call it grace. Even in the middle of some otherwise very traumatic and bewildering times, there was a sense that we were all in this fight together.

And the Scripture was our grounding rod, and reminded us of this truth. Through it, God was always sending the message to us: the forces that are *for us* are *far greater* than those that are against us. (2 Kings 6:16-17, Romans 8:31, 1 John 4:4).

I want to let you into our hearts a little. For us, the way we moved through this trial had everything to do with *honoring our Jesus* and *loving our Judah*. We did this the very best we knew how, surrendering our hearts in response to what we saw in Scripture.

We could not have walked through this without God, His grace, His Word.

From the moment Judah was born, we wholeheartedly loved, accepted, embraced and celebrated our little boy. Completely and fully. We received him as a gift from God. We also hit our knees praying for God to lead us as parents. We lifted our son up to God, knowing Judah ultimately belonged to Him.

We also believed that *Judah* was so much more than anything that his body might go through on this earth. In God's Word, we saw that *true life* is ultimately found in eternity in Christ, and all of our lives on this earth are a brief moment in comparison to the resurrection life that's to come. Our awareness of and gratitude for this hope deepened profoundly during our time with Judah.

At the same time, a resolve came over us to believe that our God is ever the life-giver and miracle-worker, and that He can do anything. In fact, we saw how Jesus *had done everything.* In God's Word, we saw our Father's heart for complete wholeness and restoration, on earth as it is in Heaven, and saw how dearly Jesus paid for it all at the Cross. *What an immeasurable gift.*

We looked at Jesus in awe, and wondered ... how could we not honor His sacrifice with everything we had?

If God and His grace are real, then we knew, *this changes everything.*

If we were going to surrender to this fully, we knew we had to stay grounded in His truth. This is why clinging to the Word of God, and praying from it, was so crucial to us.

And you know, even if we did seem crazy at times, I will say that for the most part we had incredible support rally around us. This, too, was nothing short of God's grace.

We met some remarkable people in that NICU: people who prayed with us and used their God-given gifts and wisdom to help our son. God poured out His love through people on a daily basis there, and they were His hands and feet to us.

We also met some awesome people of faith among the families. Our roads looked slightly different sometimes, but in the end, we were *in this together*.

And there was this deep, abiding mutual respect and love for one another. In each others' eyes, we could see and recognize the look of sincere devotion, of following after God, clinging to His Word with reverence, and faithfully loving our precious children.

And we could also see and recognize the pain.

Eternal bonds are formed on the battlefield.

We would pray for one another, and we would cling to the Word together. We would share scriptures as they came to our hearts, and leave notes on each others' tables. I have such tremendous gratitude and honor for these fellow soldiers.

God encouraged us through His Word in so many powerful ways. It is amazing to reflect on. This is encouragement we needed daily, as we fought alongside our Judah, and sought to live our lives as a worshipful response to Jesus, the living Word of God. And God was faithful to provide.

We certainly encountered our share of doubts and questions we didn't know how to answer. We had plenty of stumbles and struggles, and we made our mistakes. But His grace was sufficient, and He filled our places of weakness with His strength.

We also knew there would be moments we'd probably look foolish or naive to others looking on, and we'd often be swimming against the current of opposing ideas out in the world.

But what else were we to do? Jesus was worth it all. Judah was worth it all.

So we pressed on.

The Word of God was our lifeline. And as I said, God sent plenty of reinforcements.

Friends and family, and even strangers from around the world, began to pray and send us scriptures that God would put on their hearts: to build us up and encourage us in the fight. These words came to us again and again like a dove with an olive branch in its mouth, letting us know there was hope of solid ground ahead.

One of my best friends, Forrest Harmel, sent us this awesome gift in the NICU that I will never forget. It was a leather sling and leather bag that he put together for us. Inside the bag were five smooth, round stones. On each stone was written a different word like "FAITH" or "HOPE" ... and on the other side was a scripture that went with the word.

God was sending us clues through Forrest. This was a reference to David's five smooth stones that he took into battle against Goliath, and used to defeat him by the power of the Spirit.

I got the message. Our "smooth stones" were the Word of God.

And by all appearances, this giant seemed much bigger than us. But just like David, God was with us. We were not going in unarmed. And we were not outnumbered.

God had also equipped us with all those audio Bibles and preachers I told you about. We had them ready. Sometimes we played them quietly on repeat with a little audio player, right near Judah's isolette. I think we might have scared a couple of nurses, who wondered why they were hearing whispering voices at night when they walked toward his bedside.

We all had a good laugh about it later.

We posted scriptures all over our little corner of the NICU. We had cards with scriptural promises written on them, and we'd speak them, sing them, pray them ... over and over and over.

Our four parents would take shifts around the clock with us. And sometimes we would take turns pacing around the isolette with those cards, speaking out the promises God had given about healing, wholeness, peace, life, and so much else. We'd thank God for what He said in Scripture.

We would pray the Word.

Through this, grace entered. Amidst very real feelings of desperation and hardship, we still saw so much of God's grace during that time. It was like watching radiant beams of light break through the dark storm clouds. His grace shifted the atmosphere.

I truly believe that His Word and His grace filled our eyes with hope that carried us through, *and also*, breathed miraculous life into this story again and again.

At the start of Judah's life, we were told that we could probably only expect him to live one week.

We were given 20 miraculous months. And we do truly consider this miraculous. We are so grateful for every day.

And one day, I believe we will see Judah again, and the completion of God's promise.

During his incredible life here on earth, Judah bravely overcame obstacles over and over. He would characteristically surprise his NICU team, who surrounded him with their expert care and support.

After 4 months there, we got to leave the hospital, and bring him home.

It was on Thanksgiving day, no less. Also on our 4th wedding anniversary.

It was so indescribably special. The perfect anniversary gift. And we were very, very thankful.

On our way out, members of the team came to us in tears, telling us things like, "You don't know what Judah's done for my faith." Oh, how powerfully God worked through this little boy, without him ever speaking a single word.

We have so many precious memories with Judah. Pages and pages full, all demonstrating the faithfulness of God.

I have to share just one more with you.

I remember one time, on another long day within the walls of the NICU, my wife whispered to our son, "God's gonna get you out of here, baby boy. And when He does, we're gonna take you to see the mountains in Colorado."

This was an act of faith. With all the constant reminders of his fragile state, it took faith to believe we'd even get the opportunity to show him the sunlight, let alone take him on a 13-hour road trip.

But by the grace of God, we got to fulfill a mother's promise.

And I'll never forget the tears of joy that filled our eyes, when we walked out those double doors at the hospital entrance, and sunlight touched our Judah's face for the first time ...

Or the tears that flowed when his little fingers touched grass for the first time, in a lush green meadow at Glen Eyrie Castle in Colorado Springs.

My goodness. The stories go on and on ... But what I want to emphasize is this:

God is faithful. And our entire journey with Judah is filled with moments of Him lighting our path, especially with His Word.

On those long, dark nights – *and they were all long, dark nights* – His Word was the lamp that showed us where to take the next step, and His grace gave us the strength to do it. Sometimes the next step was all we could see in front of us ... but He was always faithful, and He always lit the way ...

Even in the moments we thought there was no way forward. There always was. God always made a way.

On March 29, 2019, our Judah passed away.

Judah had been embraced into eternity, into the arms of our Father in Heaven. We deeply believed he was at peace.

Still. The experience shook us in a way I don't yet know how to put into words.

The same God who held our Judah was holding us, as we faced the next level of shell shock and next layer of darkness.

Grief.

We wondered how we were going to do it. *But Jesus met us here.*

Time and time again, in so many ways, God showed He was present with us. He reached in with His amazing grace, and supernaturally carried us.

And the Word of God continued to light up our path.

Remember earlier, when I mentioned my buddy, Forrest?

When he heard the news of Judah's passing, we got on the phone and he listened to my broken father's heart. Suddenly faced with letting go, yet still wanting so much to give everything we could to our boy. We were still filled with that determined love.

Well, Forrest is also a master woodworker. He heard my heart, and in his faithful love, he stayed up all night to craft a little casket for my son's body.

It was perfect. A vessel fit for a prince. Forrest used rich wood he had saved from the prayer-filled pews of an old church. It was sturdy, and finished with the finest detail.

We placed our Judah in this beautiful casket, which was then placed in a vault. It was all too sacred not to guard.

On the top of the casket, Forrest inscribed his name:

"Judah Michael Priour"

... and right underneath: "Our Little Hero" ...

On the sides, he inscribed two scriptures that marked Judah's life.

Yes, Judah's spirit is in Heaven, and I do believe that's what really matters. And yet, this was holy. Judah was God's gift, and there was something so powerful about our son's earthly body being surrounded by Scripture. It was an act of worship, and knowing it brings a certain peace.

God did something else in this act, too. It's as if the words inscribed on Judah's casket were also inscribed on our hearts. These scriptures would become light and life, and mark us in the days to come.

The two scriptures inscribed on either side of my son's casket are Jeremiah 29:11 and 2 Timothy 4:7 (BSB). We chose them very intentionally:

> For I know the plans I have for you, declares the LORD, plans to prosper you and not to harm you, to give you a future and a hope.

> I have fought the good fight, I have finished the race, I have kept the faith.

This is the Word of the Lord. This is what we still believe.

Nothing that happens in this life can ever take away from what is eternally true.

> The Light shines in the darkness, and the darkness has not overcome it. *(John 1:5, BSB)*

2

WATER AND BREAD IN THE DESERT

My flesh and my heart fail; But God is the strength of my heart and my portion forever. *(Psalm 73:26, NKJV)*

Still. The day we had to bury our son in the ground is one I'll never forget.

We carried on. Again, by the grace of God.

Though, I'll be honest, some days felt very bleak.

I had been a preacher for nine years, and had seen God's faithfulness through my life. He'd walked me through plenty of messes, and I could remember how I used to have this fire for life.

But the passion to do much of anything was fading.

It all seemed like such a struggle to me. In our fight to have a family, with Judah, and the miscarriages. In our marriage. In our life purpose. Some days, it seemed as though my whole life had been a struggle. And I wondered why.

On those days, I saw everything through the dark and dull lens of my pain, anger, and fear. These clouded my interpretation of reality, life, people ... myself ... God ...

On those days, any vibrance in life seemed to drain away, to a dim black and white.

Inside of me, there was an inner battle. I didn't want to be this way. Theologically, I didn't blame God for any destruction that happened in Judah's life, and I genuinely believed in the profound hope flowing forth from the resurrected Christ. And I still believed that somehow, somewhere inside me, my spirit was alive and willing in Christ ...

But my heart felt very, very tired.

God continued to faithfully lift our heads, and over time, we started to stand to our feet again. The sun did rise, our smiles did return, and we did see the color come back into the picture.

God put powerful resources in our path that gave us new life, time and time again. Even though there have been many hard days, God has never stopped showing up with His resurrection life.

And again, the Word of God came to light the way.

One moment in particular comes to mind.

In those times, I remember the constant reverb of pain that pulsed in the air. I wanted to just get past it, but it seemed like it was everywhere. Some days, the sun seemed somehow too bright, and the winds felt too harsh against my face to even step outside. Sometimes, I would feel so little energy, it felt like all I could do was move just one finger.

Well, God met me right there, right where I was at. I happened to remember this phone app that a friend had recommended some time ago. At the simple click of a button, it would read scriptures aloud in a soothing voice, with the sound of the ocean underneath it.

One day, I remember sitting in my parked car in the heat of the afternoon, across from my son's private grave site at the top of a hill. I was listening to the Scripture fill the car, as I stared blankly into space. I wish I could tell you differently, but candidly: I felt dead inside that day.

Suddenly, my heart was gripped and my attention seized ... as the calming voice of the narrator brought these words from the prophet Elijah gently to my ears:

> ... he went on a day's journey into the wilderness. He sat down under a broom
> tree and prayed that he might die. He said, "I have had enough! Lord, take my

life, for I'm no better than my fathers." Then he lay down and slept under the broom tree ... *(1 Kings 19:4-5, HCSB)*

Right at that moment, I looked up and saw an oak tree in front of me. This tree was very special. It provided dappled shade over my son's grave and the sitting area next to it. And today was one of those brutal Texas days, when the heat was beating down relentlessly, and the sun seemed just a bit too bright ...

I suddenly imagined the tree that Elijah found in the wilderness, and saw him collapsing under it after a long day of running away from life. And I heard his words of utter defeat.

I mean, *I really heard them.*

I connected with Elijah. Those words resonated so deeply in my heart, and my eyes began to fill with tears, which strangely offered a moment of deep relief from the numbness I was used to living in.

"I've had enough," I thought out loud, in a whisper. "I don't want to go on."

I took a deep breath, and could feel my breath shake under the crushing weight that sat on my chest. The narrator continued to tell the story.

While Elijah was sleeping, an angel came to him and touched him.

> ... The angel told him, "Get up and eat." Then he looked, and there at his head was a loaf of bread baked over hot stones, and a jug of water. So he ate and drank and lay down again. *(1 Kings 19:5-6, HCSB)*

God had come to replenish Elijah in the middle of his sleep. And after a while of more sleeping, the angel came back a second time to bring him more sustenance, and said:

> "Arise and eat, because the journey is too great for you." *(1 Kings 19:7, HCSB)*

And there I was, lying in my car, feeling like I was sleepwalking through life, and wanting to run away from it all.

The journey was too great for me. I couldn't do it alone.

And I wasn't alone. I never had been, no matter how much I might have felt it.

And God, in His grace, continued to send me the food and water I needed for my soul to be revived.

That afternoon, I think I might have actually fallen asleep right there in the car a few times, drifting in and out of consciousness. Each time I woke, I'd hit the button on my phone again, and God would give me more life from the water of His Spirit, and feed me the sweet bread of His Word.

This particular phone app had scriptures grouped together by theme, and so this story was grouped with other verses. I had clicked the buttons for "weary" and "beaten" – which were filled with scriptures to listen to when you felt these ways ... and I certainly did.

One of the narrated verses was very familiar to me, but that day, these words of Jesus hit me in a way I'd never felt before:

"Come to me, all you who are weary and burdened, and I will give you rest. Take my yoke upon you and learn from me, for I am gentle and humble in heart, and you will find rest for your souls. For my yoke is easy and my burden is light." *(Matthew 11:28-30, NIV)*

Suddenly, it felt as though the voice was now narrating what was happening to me in this moment. And I began to speak out what I was hearing.

I prayed the Word.

"Jesus, I'm weary. I'm coming to You, asking for Your rest for my soul ..."

A simple act of trust, moved by His amazing grace. One that opened the door for grace to flow in.

Oh, thank You, precious Jesus.

Verse by verse, wave after wave, the Word continued to wash over me, like the ocean that undergirded the narrator's voice.

It was as if His grace was slowly filling the car. The weight began to lift off my chest. I began to sense the presence of God with me.

And I began to feel hope again.

Maybe in the moment, it might have *seemed* small in comparison to everything else I was feeling. Well actually, in the moment, there was a greatness about it.

It felt eternal.

I suppose what I mean is: I knew there was still life to face outside my car. And this hope might have appeared to me like a cloud the size of a man's fist in a vast open sky, in the middle of the desert, in the middle of a drought …

But there was rain in that cloud.

God came through. When the journey was too great for me, he provided me with food and water for my soul. He gave me life and vision again. Bite by bite. Drink by drink. Step by step.

There was still a journey ahead, rife with challenges. And I still had a lot of pain to face. I still had lies to release, and truth to embrace. I still do.

But I remember this day as a turning point, when the Word of the Lord came to me, like rain in a drought. Like a cloud to cover by day, and a light to shine at night.

Like bread and water in the desert.

In the Bible account that I mentioned, Elijah rose up again, and he was able to travel 40 days and 40 nights on the strength of the food that God provided him from Heaven.

So too, the water of His Spirit and bread of His Word filled me with supernatural strength I cannot explain.

In his journey, Elijah would go on to encounter God, who spoke truth and clarity into Elijah's heart, in a "still, small voice" (1 Kings 19:12).

So too, God spoke to me in the stillness, in the quiet of my heart.

In returning and rest was my salvation. In quietness and trust was my strength. (Isaiah 30:15).

Faith came to me by hearing, and hearing by the Word of God. (Romans 10:17).

And when His words came to me, I ate them, and they were my joy and my heart's delight. (Jeremiah 15:16).

From His fullness I received what I needed. Grace upon Grace. (John 1:16).

He satisfied my longing soul, and filled my hungry soul with goodness. (Psalm 107:9).

And Jesus kept His promise. I came to Him weary and burdened. And He gave me rest for my soul. (Matthew 11:28-30).

As I come to Him more, I become more convinced of His words. He is truly gentle and humble in heart. I continue to learn from Him, how to take up His easy yoke, and light burden. And as I do, I continue to find the rest that my soul has needed all along.

And I continue to encounter more deeply what I did that day, when God met me by my son's grave: that which has *always* been true:

Our God is so, so good. *Thank You, precious Jesus.*

I would have lost heart, unless I had believed that I would see the goodness of the LORD In the land of the living. *(Psalm 27:13, NKJV)*

Taste and see that the Lord is good. Oh, the joys of those who take refuge in him! *(Psalm 34:8, NLT)*

Give thanks to the LORD, for He is good; His loving devotion endures forever. *(1 Chronicles 16:34, BSB)*

And the LORD passed before him and proclaimed, "The LORD, the LORD God, merciful and gracious, longsuffering, and abounding in goodness and truth." *(Exodus 34:6, NKJV)*

The LORD is good to everyone. He showers compassion on all his creation. *(Psalm 145:9, NLT)*

Oh, that men would give thanks to the Lord for His goodness, and for His wonderful works to the children of men! For He satisfies the longing soul, and fills the hungry soul with goodness. *(Psalm 107:8-9, NKJV)*

Surely your goodness and love will follow me all the days of my life, and I will dwell in the house of the LORD forever. *(Psalm 23:6, NIV)*

3

REMEMBERING THE GOODNESS OF GOD

Return to your rest, my soul, for the LORD has been good to you. (Psalm 116:7, NIV)

My wife and I have loved to lead worship together. One of our all-time favorite songs is "Goodness of God" by Jenn Johnson[1]. It's a beautiful song, marveling at God's unfailing love, goodness, and faithfulness which has been present through all our lives. My wife thinks of it as her own life anthem.

It was released the same year Judah passed away. I remember showing it to Faith for the first time, and her description of hearing it. She was struck by the truth in the words ... yet she felt this sharp sting in her heart as she heard them, because of all that we had faced.

We have resolved that the truth about God must be defined by Jesus, who is the only visible image of the invisible God. Jesus is the Rock: sturdy and consistent. We must trust how God reveals Himself, over and above any of our own feelings or experiences, which are tumultuous and unsteady.

I absolutely believe God cares for our hearts more than we could imagine. At the same time, if our hearts tell us a contrary story to God's reality revealed in Christ and Scripture: God is greater than our hearts.

And our hurting hearts have encountered God's light through this song many times: in all His pure truth and goodness, overflowing grace, and perfect love.

There's something about music that can stir the waters of the heart in a way nothing else can. This worship song was filled with Scriptural truths and phrases, and the beauty of the music resonated with the truth in our spirits.

The truth that God has been faithful and good for our entire lives. The truth revealed in Scripture:

> Give thanks to the LORD, for he is good!
>
> His faithful love endures forever. *(Psalm 136:1, NLT)*
>
> ... For His faithfulness is everlasting. *(Psalm 136:1, NASB)*

This music also made its way past our walls, striking the chords of pain points buried deep within our hurting hearts, and revealing the dissonance between *what we felt* and *what is true*.

We've learned to lean into these moments, lay our feelings before God openly and honestly. God can handle it, and I believe He even wants it. *All of it.*

I see David doing this in the Psalms, along with many other figures in the Bible. I see them openly processing their hurt, disillusionment, weariness, fear, and so on.

And at the end of his Psalms, after all the processing, David still reaches beyond the feelings to declare what is true of God. In all of this, David was called "a man after God's own heart."

Well, when Faith heard this song, it called her name. She immediately felt called to learn it. Not long after, she wanted to lead it in a worship set at church. Yet her heart wrestled through it with God, just like David. She said openly at one point, "I don't feel like singing this song," because her soul had also become very tired, and very weighed down with the hurt of loss.

I'll never forget watching her rise up and sing it anyway. It was absolutely anointed. I've heard her sing that song over and over at different places throughout these last years. I have seen both her and the crowds weeping, as she declared before people needing hope: that no matter what we have felt or gone through, God's truth and faithfulness have always remained the same.

She is a woman after God's own heart.

God is greater than our feelings or our interpretation of reality. And He is always and forever good.

The chorus ends with the *all-in* surrendered declaration, that we will declare the goodness of God with every breath we have to give …

This is our story, this is our song.

Yes, and it is absolutely true. He has been faithful for all our lives. He has always been good to us. And it is well with our souls.

And this song, filled with Scriptural truth, came to light our path and revive our hearts, when we needed it most. And every time we sang it, we were praying and communing with His truth, becoming more grounded in it.

It compelled us to go to the bookshelves, reach for our Bibles, and pray the Word again.

We prayed the Scripture, inscribed on the sides of Judah's casket, and on our hearts … thanking God for His good plans to give us a future and a hope. We prayed for strength to fight the good fight, and finish our race. We resolved to keep the faith.

And next to Jesus, Judah was our inspiration. *Our little hero.*

In light of God's grace, and all He has done, *what else were we to do?*

Jesus was worth it all. Judah was worth it all.

So we pressed on.

We continued, and trusted God. We believed God's good plans for our family were not over. Despite all that had happened, we continued to believe and receive the Word of God, and it worked powerfully in us.

I saw my wife truly live out the meaning of her name. She did not give up. She kept the faith. And there would definitely be challenges ahead, that knocked us back and shook us. But we got back up, dusted off, and held onto God and the word of His amazing grace.

And what can I say, except: God is faithful. God is good.

We have a second son now, named Miles. He's 2 years old as I write this. The worship song was playing in the delivery room the moment he was born.

He has a little sister due in a few months. Right now, we're thinking of naming her Mercy.

It's by God's unfailing Mercy that we've come this far. And it has been a journey of many Miles, one that God has faithfully walked with us the whole way.

And both of our children are perfectly healthy, by God's amazing grace.

Miles is the absolute joy of our lives. He loves to look at pictures of his "Bubba Judah" and hear his stories.

As I type this, he is actually out in the living room with his mama, laughing and squealing and running laps around the kitchen, flailing his arms and "doing exercise" while listening to his favorite worship songs.

He really likes fire trucks, helicopters, cars and choo choo trains. And also Christmas trees. He doesn't like dirt under his nails and doesn't like having to wait for hot pizza to cool down. He enjoys feeding ducks by the river, putting together puzzles, and making snowmen out of play dough.

He loves his family. He loves wrestling with Daddy and laying his head on Daddy's shoulder. He loves being held in Mommy's arms. He loves it when we sing him songs.

And he loves songs about Jesus.

We have made a lot of wonderful memories together, and have gone through a lot of true, deep healing. We are excited about the destiny God has for our children's lives. And we watch in awe at how our Judah's legacy still carries forth, even past his earthly life.

I love you, little buddy. God, I'm so proud of you. See? You inspired Daddy to write a book. Maybe Jesus will tell you all about it.

It is absolutely miraculous how far God has taken us. For a moment there, we weren't sure we were ever going to get back up.

We might have lost heart, had we not believed we would see the goodness of God in the land of the living.

And the whole time, God has lovingly reminded us of who He is through His Word. His promises. His goodness. His grace.

In so many creative, powerful ways.

I'll say it again. *I don't know where we would be without the grace of God. And I don't know where we would be without His Word.*

~

Which brings me to today.

Why did I write this book?

I wrote the book that I would have wanted on this journey. The book I would have wanted on my nightstand. And actually, the one I want on my nightstand *now*.

I have needed a lot of reminding of who God is, and all He has done by His grace. Not just in the wake of our son's passing. I have needed His breath of life, and His amazing grace, every day I've spent on this earth.

And what's more, it has always been there for me, in overflowing abundance. Though I often did not know this, it's always been true.

Sometimes I have wanted to have a book by my side, packed with scriptures and prayers, that dove into a theme in depth. Like I would do with my laminated pages in the shower. Like those precious scriptures that came to me that afternoon by my son's grave. Like a worship song, written on a beautiful aspect of God's nature.

So I did it. I dove in myself, and I wrote the book. I may be new to this, but this work comes from many years of digging for God's precious truth. And I am putting it out there so that maybe it could bless someone else, too.

You never know when God's lamp will arise at just the right time, to shine a light in the darkness.

Here's another reason why I want this book on my nightstand.

The Scripture says this about itself:

All Scripture is God-breathed and is useful for teaching, rebuking, correcting and training in righteousness, so that the servant of God may be thoroughly equipped for every good work. *(2 Timothy 3:16-17, NIV)*

The Scripture is breathed out by the very breath of God. Do you remember what the breath of God did with dust in Genesis?

Then the LORD God formed a man from the dust of the ground and breathed into his nostrils the breath of life, and the man became a living being. *(Genesis 2:7, NIV)*

God's Word breathes life into the dust. It resurrects, renews, and restores. It lights our path in the darkness. It revives and refreshes the soul, and it is health to our bones.

It washes and cleanses us (Ephesians 5:26, John 15:3). It is alive and powerful (Hebrews 4:12), and it always produces fruit (Isaiah 55:11).

There is so much power available in the Scripture, that is ours to take hold of. It's already been given.

But we must take hold. That's our part.

I will admit to you. My faith has many times felt tired. Even to the point where it felt like the flame had burned out entirely.

But God gives more grace. He provides more oil for the lamp to burn. He just keeps bringing life. It's who He is. It's what He does.

And miraculously, the flame is still here.

Now, fanning the flame has taken some action on my part. Make no mistake: it was His strength, His power, His grace at work within me. But faith is animated by *action*.

It took me bringing all of my honest, ugly, raw feelings before the throne of grace and letting Him into those places. I wept plenty, and even screamed at times, until I was lying on the floor with nothing left. I poured out everything to Him, even processing the moments when it felt like I had taken a leap and *it felt like* no one caught me. I cried out in the unknowing, and spent myself at His throne.

And the amazing thing is, as I poured out my heart and trusted Him with all of it ... guess whose arms I always found myself falling into? Guess who was there to lift my head? He *always* caught me. I was never turned away, not once. I was always embraced by a loving Father. And I always received the amazing grace I needed, even if it took time to work out or realize.

This faith journey meant me wrestling with these words in Scripture when I felt internal dissonance; crying out, just like the father who brought his hurting son to Jesus: "I do believe, but help me overcome my unbelief!" (Mark 9:24, NLT)

It also took me looking beyond whatever I felt and returning to the truth: God has been good to me. Goodness is simply who He is. I was never alone, or abandoned. He had always been there for me, and He had always caught me. Even in times that I wasn't able to see it, when fear shrouded my vision, He never left my side (Deuteronomy 31:8).

All my life, He has been faithful, and so, so good.

It took me trusting the Father's heart, and responding to His invitation. It took coming to the river of life and drinking freely from it, feeding on the daily bread He gives, and resting my soul in Him.

It took trusting that Jesus really is who He says He is.

Somewhere deep down I've known ... that no feeling, or lack of faith in me, or anyone, would ever be able nullify the faithfulness of God (Romans 3:3-4, 2 Timothy 2:13). He is still the truth. Let God be true, and everything else be a lie. His words are pure and tested. He cannot deny Himself.

And He can breathe life on anything. He is still, and forever, the one who gives life (John 10:10).

And God has revived me. *I still believe.* And my goodness ... even this is a work of His grace, and because of His faithfulness. I truly have nothing to boast about in myself.

I am thankful for life experiences, and in a way, they do shape us. I am grateful for all that has led me to this point.

And yet, my prayer has been that I would not adjust my belief system to fit my experience, story, or feelings. But rather, to be adjusted by God and His consistent truth.

Here's a simple illustration that might help.

For about half of the time I live, I don't see the sun. The reason is simple. This is because it's night time, and it's on the other side of the earth. I don't conclude that the sun must be shutting off, simply because I don't see it for that time.

In fact, I've got a few friends on the other side of the world who can confirm with a simple phone call that the sun is still on. They can feel its warmth in times I can't.

No, the sun never changes: only my experience of it does. The sun is still shining constantly and faithfully. I'm the one on a rotating and shifting earth. And I can close my eyes, or hide under a blanket, or live in a cave under the earth and never experience its warmth. *But the sun still goes on shining,* and the truth remains the same, no matter what my subjective experience is.

I am here to step into the sun, and submit myself to be transformed by God and His Word, and become deeply rooted in His truth. Even greater than the sun, God is everywhere all the time. The light of His truth is constant, and it is so, so good. And when we know the truth for ourselves, it sets us free (John 8:32).

This is another reason I wrote this book: to become more grounded in the grace and truth of Jesus Christ, and God's reality, which may be greater and more real than the one we see with our eyes.

I remember as a kid, being taught how to walk on a balance beam. I was told to find a stable point to focus on in front of me, to keep from falling off. Focusing on the unstable world around us can make us stumble, and make us forget ... *just how glorious and steadfast God and His reality are.*

The apostles encountered the Living Word, Jesus Christ Himself. And they saw something that gave them tremendous stability and peace, even in the face of death. They said:

> The sufferings of this present time are not worthy to be compared with the glory which shall be revealed in us. *(Romans 8:18, KJV)*

This means there is glory to behold, friend, and it far surpasses any pain we will ever experience in this world. Jesus said to us:

> These things I have spoken to you, that in Me you may have peace. In the world you will have tribulation; but be of good cheer, I have overcome the world. (*John 16:33, NKJV*)

This present world comes with troubles. That's just part of the package. I hope you can see by now I'm not trying to gloss over that.

But if the Word He speaks is true – and I believe it is – then we can truly, actually take heart in Him. We can be of good cheer, for He has overcome the world. This brings tremendous peace.

And once more, I am not denying the hurt or trouble. I'm learning to be very honest with God about that.

But I am also not denying the unexplainable, miraculous joy found in Christ. Or the rest that we find for our souls when we come to Him with our burdens. And the peace of God that transcends all understanding.

This is the peace that comes to us when we bring everything to His throne of grace without reservation; and saturate ourselves in what is true, receive His grace by faith, and live our lives from everything God has given and said (Philippians 4:6-9).

And all of this is found in Christ, who is full of grace and truth.

Up until this point, I have used "Scripture" and "God's Word" interchangeably, and for the sake of this book, will probably continue to at times.

However, I do ultimately believe that Jesus Himself is the true and living "Word of God" (John 1:1). I don't want to miss that. It is in praying through the God-breathed Scripture, that I have encountered the Living Word, *who is* God. It was then that my heart was transformed, my path was lit, I received life, and the purpose of this exercise was fulfilled.

In the end, I believe He is the very reason for life itself. He is life itself! He is the truth. He is the way. (John 14:6).

I have found the words of St. Augustine to be true:

You have made us for yourself, O Lord, and our heart is restless until it rests in you.

— *St Augustine of Hippo*[2]

In all the restless questioning of my heart, God Himself has been the answer I have been looking for all along. My heart finds its rest in *Him*.

In the trials I have experienced ... He is still the answer.

We live in a world where there is brokenness, and honestly there could be a million reasons why any one tragic thing happens. Most likely, it's a whole mix of things accumulated that lead up to any event in this world.

This isn't a philosophy or theology book, per se. I humbly admit that I stand among giants in the faith who have spent their lives writing such great works in those categories. This book is not about throwing my hat in that ring.

All I am saying is, I have personally concluded that I don't need to know all the reasons why something happened, and I'm not sure I ever could without being Almighty God. God will show me what He wants to show me, and lead me down the paths He wants me to take.

God is faithful. And honestly, He has revealed to us some awesome, life-giving wisdom to help us learn and draw life from these experiences, and go on to help others. I won't deny that, and I am very grateful for all of it.

But as for my core beliefs, where my heart rests, where my identity and way of being come from ... I simply cannot build my house on the shifting sands of circumstance or human wisdom. I choose to build on the Rock of Christ.

So, "return to your rest, my soul, for the Lord has been good to you." I return to the goodness of God. I listen again to what He has said, abiding and continuing in His Word.

I will also say, that I am aware of my humanness, and the limits of my experience and understanding. I know I will see things imperfectly in this life (1 Corinthians 13:12).

Remember Glen Eyrie Castle, where we took Judah to in Colorado? That was actually our third time to go, and we've gone a couple times since. We just love it. I remember when my wife first found the place online, for our first anniversary trip. The pictures were absolutely stunning. But no picture could ever replicate the full glorious experience of actually being there. I remember us actually crying tears of joy when we first drove through the gates.

In a similar way, I have pictures of God's glory, through Scripture and personal experiences with God and His grace. And they are nothing short of breathtaking. But there will be things I miss, and nothing will compare with the full unveiling we will someday see.

What I do, is I fix my eyes on Jesus, cling to His Word, and run my race *with all I've got* (Hebrews 12:2, Philippians 3:12-16). I pray for God to lead me in His truth (Psalms 25:5), and the trust Holy Spirit to faithfully do just that (John 16:13), as I continue to work out my own salvation (Philippians 2:12).

I have a new friend, Dan. We were just having coffee, and he described to me his theology as sometimes being like a messy desk of papers. Sometimes, he'll add another note here, or scrap that one there, and rearrange the order of the notes. I so relate to this.

There are no doubt some key core beliefs in our faith, agreed upon in creeds through the centuries. Those pages get stapled to the desk. But we are growing, learning human beings. My beliefs are living and breathing, and I'm still working things out with God. I'm not at the same place I was years ago. God is absolutely consistent. But I have grown, and will continue to.

Knowing I see in part, feeling like I'm shuffling through papers and pictures on my messy desk to try to figure out which ones to put in here, and aware I won't be able to really capture all the layers ...

With all that said, in the spirit of opening my journey to you, I want to share a few glimpses into what I've come to see. Honestly, as I share this, I marvel. The fact that I still believe this way, let alone write a book to tell about it, is evidence to me of the power of His Word and grace at work in my life.

This faith is the substance of things hoped for. The evidence of things not seen. (Hebrews 11:1).

I still believe the day is coming when:

... God will wipe away every tear from their eyes; there shall be no more death, nor sorrow, nor crying. There shall be no more pain, for the former things have passed away. *(Revelation 21:4, NKJV)*

I have this hope as an anchor for my soul.

In that glorious day, who knows the magnitude of the wonderful things we will see? As it is written:

For now we see only a reflection as in a mirror; then we shall see face to face. Now I know in part; then I shall know fully, even as I am fully known. *(1 Corinthians 13:12, NIV)*

Oh the glory, of seeing Jesus face to face, in perfect clarity ... of knowing Him fully, even as I am fully known ... I can only imagine. Perhaps we'll cry tears of joy as we drive through the gates ...

And perhaps on that day, the questions I had in this life won't even matter anymore. Perhaps they will fade away in the glorious light of the Son.

Until then, Jesus Himself is still the Resurrection and the Life (John 11:25). He is raised from the dead and seated on a Heavenly throne forever ... and *on our behalf*, having united us with Him. That picture alone is breathtaking ...

I'll go on by saying what I said before: I believe our *true life* is found in the priceless gift of eternity in Christ, beyond this momentary breath of time we have in earthen vessels right now.

I will also reiterate that during our time with Judah, our awareness and gratitude for this *greater reality* deepened in a way I cannot describe. I believe that Judah is whole. What incredible hope and peace accompany this belief. I believe that, in a way, Judah is more alive now than he was on earth. And, he is more at home.

It *truly is* well with my soul.

And there is yet more to come: In the twinkling of an eye, when the dead in Christ are raised in the Resurrection, clothed with immortality, and Life is fully realized (1 Corinthians 15). *"O death, where is your sting?"*

At this moment, Jesus is eternally seated in majesty, as King over all. From His perspective, life and death no doubt look very different than how we tend to see them. Those who caught His vision, called the sufferings of the present life a "light, momentary affliction," and "not worthy to be compared with the glory that is about to be revealed to us and in us" (2 Corinthians 4:17, Romans 8:18).

And at the same time, I still believe that the God I worship is a God of miracles, who works just as powerfully today as He did in the days that Jesus walked the earth (Psalm 77:14, John 14:12). And this is to the glory of God. I don't believe He has withheld any gift (Romans 11:29), and I believe that everything for healing, wholeness, life and godliness, was provided in Christ, through His accomplished, atoning work. (Isaiah 53:4-5, 1 Peter 2:24, John 19:30).

And also, I still believe in a God who masterfully brings the most incredible good out of the most tragic situations (Genesis 50:20, Romans 8:28) ... A God who gives beauty for ashes, joy for mourning, and praise for despair (Isaiah 61:3) ... A God who takes the filth and the mud, and uses the very same for rich soil, in which He plants the most beautiful gardens.

This too is nothing short of miraculous. He is a redeeming genius, and wastes nothing. I stand amazed at how He still uses *all* of Judah's story to bring incredible glory and hope.

In God's magnificent beauty, this is all somehow concurrently true.

And while God does make beautiful things out of the dust, in a way that only God can ... I still do not draw the conclusion that He was the source of calamity. The glory I see when I look at Jesus simply does not allow me to, even in the face of questions I still don't have answers to. Jesus is Life. I can't un-see it. I cannot tell you how much this revelation has formed me ...

Here is a brief glimpse into some of what I see when I behold the Son of God.

I see that Jesus is the one and only *definitive* revelation of God, the "visible image of the invisible", the "exact representation of God's being", the Only Son and the *only one* who reveals the Father to us. When we see Him, we see the Father. (John 1:1, Colossians 1:15, Hebrews 1:3, John 1:14;18, John 14:7-9, Matthew 11:27).

It's the thief who comes only to steal, kill, and destroy; Jesus came to give us abundant life, to the very fullest. Jesus is the life-giver, who came to save lives and not destroy them, bringing the very life of Heaven to earth. He illuminated the way to life and immortality through the gospel, destroying the power of death. (John 10:10, John 3:16-17, Luke 9:56, John 6:33, Matthew 6:10, 2 Timothy 1:9-10).

Jesus is also the Triumphant One over *all* the opposing forces of darkness, including the "enemy" of death itself. (1 John 3:8, Acts 10:38, John 12:31, John 14:30, John 1:5, Colossians 2:15, Hebrews 2:14-15, 1 Corinthians 15:26, 2 Timothy 1:10).

While we do live in a world where there is still pain, Jesus has already overcome the world. There is a *greater reality* than what our natural eyes can see, and by faith in Christ, we are interwoven with Him and His reality. From Heaven's vantage point, the victory is already ours in Christ (1 Corinthians 15:57, 2 Corinthians 2:14, 1 John 5:4, Romans 8:31, Hebrews 2:8-9, 1 Peter 2:24, Colossians 3:1-4, Ephesians 2:5-6, John 16:63, Revelation 1:18).

The people who saw Jesus for themselves told us, "Now this is the message we have heard from Him and declare to you: God is light, and there is absolutely no darkness in Him." (1 John 1:5, HCSB).

In short, while I certainly don't have all the answers, when I look at the brokenness of this world: it is not God's fingerprints that I find on the smoking gun at the scene of the crime.

You know where I do see His fingerprints?

On the torturous crossbeam that Jesus held onto tightly, as He carried my cross through the streets and up to Calvary. I see them on the nails he gripped while hanging there to die my death for me. I see His fingerprints all over the places where Christ stood in my place, and where he took me by the hand to lead me into the eternal glory of new life in Him.

I find the fingerprints everywhere that my Father, in His relentless love, searched for me in the night of my own darkness. Or I find them wrapped around me, in the places my Father held me in His loving embrace, and on His best robes He threw around me to clothe me, after I came home exhausted from a long journey of running away (Luke 15:20).

I see the hand of God where the Holy Spirit worked His wonders and miracles, and cast out the darkness with His invincible light. Surely *this* was the "finger of God" (Luke 11:20).

I see God in the hands of the nurses and doctors who cared for our son, and the friends and family who reached out with compassion and grace to lift us when we were down.

Everywhere I find pure light, life and love: those are the places I find God in the story.

And all of this is only scratching the surface of how God's plan is intricately good, how life gets the last word in Christ, and how His goodness and grace permeate our world in which we live. It is right at our fingertips to grasp by faith in Christ, just beyond the veil of what our natural eyes can see.

I could go on, but I guess this subject is far too complex to peel open here. Nor is it really the purpose of this book ...

My goal here is to tell you of how I've made it my aim to return to His Word in the face of trials, and reach for His truth. Also, to marvel at how faithful God has been to revive my heart with His Word and His grace.

Here is something a little more on topic of this book:

I still believe all of the promises in Scripture are true. I still believe in these words that I've gathered together in this book, and crafted into prayers.

I believe God's Word is settled in Heaven forever (Psalm 119:89). I believe His promises are all "Yes" in Christ (2 Corinthians 1:20), and that they are for here and now, on earth as it is in Heaven (Matthew 6:10). Jesus Christ is the same yesterday, today, and forever (Hebrews 13:8). He has finished the work of redemption (John 19:30), and today is the day to take hold of grace. Today is the day of salvation (2 Corinthians 6:2).

I believe the Word of God is living and active (Hebrews 4:12), and more real than anything in this world. In fact, I believe that the world itself is held together by the Word of His power (Hebrews 1:3).

And here's something else that I believe could very well be true.

I wonder if much of our life in Christ – if not all of it – is coming to realize what God has already done in His grace, and learning to receive it by faith (Romans

5:2).

And from that place, we live our life in Christ by taking action in response to Him, and that's when He truly breathes His life into our experience.

In Christ, God has already freely given and provided everything we will ever need for life in Him (2 Peter 1:3).

This is grace.

Our part now is to receive grace by faith. To do like my mentor D. W. Martin has taught me: *to take hold of that* for which *Christ took hold of us* (Philippians 3:12). This is the purpose of this book.

So, friend.

These are just a few of my stories that illustrate God showing up in my time of need. I wanted to share them, so you can know where I'm coming from.

I am just a fellow traveler on the road, with plenty to learn. I am still on the journey of, *"I believe. Help my unbelief."* And I am so eager to know God more, and fully embrace Christ and His grace, as Christ has fully embraced me.

My hope in writing this book is that we might saturate ourselves in God's Word, and do just that.

I have come to see the power of echoing His Word back to Him in prayers of faith. I believe that when we do that, we can come to know the God of grace more and more, access His grace which He has freely given, and invite His Spirit to move in our lives in greater measure.

And now you know a little bit of why that idea moves me so much.

I have focused this book on the theme of God's grace. Perhaps my story speaks for itself as to why I made that choice.

But just in case you are hungry for more, I want to elaborate on the theme of grace in the coming sections. May these next chapters stir up excitement and encouragement for our journey ahead, and get our hearts set on our prize: to know God, and His glorious grace.

> "Now this is eternal life: that they know you, the only true God, and Jesus Christ, whom you have sent." *(John 17:3, NIV)*

"... grow in the grace and knowledge of our Lord and Savior Jesus Christ. To him be glory both now and forever! Amen." *(2 Peter 3:18, NIV)*

"And now I commend you to God and to the word of his grace ..." *(Acts 20:32, ESV)*

4

WHY GRACE: A MOST GLORIOUS THEME

So, why grace?

Oh my. Where to begin ...

How about here:

> Amazing grace! How sweet the sound ...[1]

How sweet the sound ...

In a symphony, a repeated musical idea or melody is called a theme.

The theme is introduced somewhere in the beginning of the symphony. Throughout all the complexity of this musical composition, the theme is repeated, since it is the most important idea of the piece.

When a composer changes the theme in different ways – such as varying time, rhythm, or tonality – but the listener can still recognize the theme: this is called a variation.

If the entire story of God and humanity were a breathtaking symphony – and it is – grace would be a major theme, with many marvelous variations throughout.

In the Holy Bible, this grand symphony has several significant movements.

From the thrilling heights found in the wonder of creation ...

To the heart-wrenching depths found in humanity's tragic fall ...

Followed by the vast emotional swells and swings found in God's great redemptive story, lived out and prophesied in God's journey with Israel ...

We hear such a dramatic spectrum of tones ... the celebration and lament ... the silent stillness and vibrant expression ... the tension and release ... the harmony and discord ... all found in the call and response of God's love song with humankind ...

Then at last, the great crescendo ... the climactic intersection of Heaven and earth ... the glorious collision where every theme plays at once in perfect harmony ... redemption's final fulfillment in the Son of God, Jesus Christ!

And the people stand to their feet with thunderous applause!

And the whole time, from start to finish, we hear a most wonderful theme. It's the riveting melody of grace: in its many marvelous variations throughout Scripture – from the subtle, to the spectacular – reaching its ecstatic pinnacle in the appearing of our Lord Jesus Christ.

One cannot read Scripture without getting the idea that "grace" is absolutely central to the story of God and us, and all of life in Christ.

Simply put, to know God is to know grace, and to know grace is to know God!

Grace is inextricably woven together with the God of Jesus Christ. Our God is a God of grace.

In fact, grace distinguishes the God we believe in.

There is a story told about C.S. Lewis (1898 – 1963), renowned British author and man of faith.[2]

He was at a British conference on comparative religions, where experts from around the world were in attendance.

As the story goes, a group of people were debating about what was unique about the Christian faith. Many suggestions were offered and rejected.

At some point, C.S. Lewis heard the discussion and interjected. *What's unique about Christianity?*

"Oh, that's easy." Lewis says. "It's grace."

We know that taking hold of grace is *indispensable* to our journey of knowing God.

Let's look at the Scripture. Briefly, here are a few things to consider:

We've been entrusted to God and to the "word of His grace" (Acts 20:32). We are urged to continue in God's grace (Acts 13:43), to grow in grace (2 Peter 3:18), have our hearts established and strengthened by grace (Hebrews 13:9), put all our hope completely in grace (1 Peter 1:13), to not ignore grace or set it aside (Galatians 2:21), and to stand firm (1 Peter 5:12) and be strong in the grace of God (2 Timothy 2:1).

And that's just the beginning of it.

The apostles gave their whole lives for this glorious "gospel of God's grace" (Acts 20:24). Grace is written all over their letters to the church. In fact:

> Paul ends his letters as he begins them, praying that grace be with those who read this letter. From first to last, the life of faith is framed by grace.
>
> — *Footnote, 2 Corinthians 13, The VOICE Translation*[3]

This theme has been the fascination of many since then. Throughout the ages, believers have heard the sweet music of God's amazing grace, and it has resonated deep within their hearts.

The celebrated minister Dr. Martin Lloyd Jones (1899 – 1981) wrote in his book, *Spiritual Depression: Its Causes and Cures*,

> The secret of a happy Christian life is to realize that it is all of grace and to rejoice in that fact ... Christian life starts with grace, it must continue with grace, it ends with grace. Grace, wondrous grace.[4]

John Newton (1725 – 1807) wrote the unforgettable hymn *Amazing Grace*, mentioned at the start of this chapter. John must have heard the sound often.

In fact, receiving God's grace ignited such gratitude in his heart, that he wrote another hymn, entitled *Reigning Grace*. In it, he writes further on the same theme:

No sweeter subject can invite

A sinner's heart to sing;

Or more display the glorious right

Of our exalted King.

This subject fills the starry plains

With wonder, joy, and love;

And furnishes the noblest strains

For all the harps above.[5]

What Heavenly music John must have heard ... He goes on to write:

'Twas grace that call'd our souls at first;

By grace thus far we're come;

And grace will help us through the worst,

And lead us safely home.

Oh the reigning grace of God, written into His symphony from start to finish!

And that's exactly what this book is about. Grace, wondrous grace.

So ... what exactly *is grace*?

Goodness. So many great people throughout time have offered definitions, from theologians and authors, to preachers and poets. I have encountered some of them, and I'm so grateful for the work of these anointed pioneers of the faith! I encourage you to seek out their work!

This book is not intended for that. I am not attempting any sort of exhaustive theological treatise, even on the topic of grace. Furthermore, this book isn't intended to cover all aspects of the life of Christ, or be a comprehensive study of God's nature, or a complete guide to Christian living.

This book is intended to be an immersive, open-hearted exploration on the theme of grace through the rich pages of Scripture. And it is an adventure we will take in communion with God through prayer.

Put simply: The intention of this book is that you would encounter God and experience His grace, through Scripture and prayer crafted from the words therein.

Ultimately, my hope is that – as we immerse ourselves in grace, lingering long at the foot of the Cross, and praying the word of His grace – we will hear for ourselves some of the variations on this beautiful theme in God's magnificent, intricate symphony.

May we hear it in the depths of our souls, friend, until we can't help but join in the timeless refrain,

Amazing grace, how sweet the sound ...

5

MY METHOD: TURNING THE DIAMOND IN THE LIGHT

In Acts 20, the apostle Paul gathered a group of elders from the church in Ephesus. It was a deeply emotional farewell to them, but this moment was also holy, and filled with purpose.

He was telling them that he was headed to Jerusalem to continue spreading the Good News, though soberly, he knew it would ultimately cost him his life.

But Paul seemed to have a certain sparkle in his eye. He was set on fire with a Heavenly calling. So he told them,

> "But none of these things move me; nor do I count my life dear to myself, so that I may finish my race with joy, and the ministry which I received from the Lord Jesus, to testify to the gospel of the grace of God." *(Acts 20:24, NKJV)*

Truly, many have given their lives over centuries so you and I could hear the Good News of God's grace. This is a powerful reality to ponder.

The Scripture says that the riches of God's grace are unsearchable: a word which indicates that we will never reach the end of them. They are unlimited, boundless, infinite. Try as we may to plumb the depths of grace, we'll never be able to measure it or conclude we've seen it all.

Although we'll never reach the end of His riches, that certainly doesn't mean we don't explore them. In fact, I believe that's the very thing God wants us to do. We will forever be freshly experiencing and unwrapping the gift He has given us!

God lovingly beckons us, through the music of His glorious gospel, into a never-ending exploration through the riches of His grace. He has invited us on a Heavenly treasure hunt! (Matthew 13:44-46).

He invites us to come and drink from the river of life (John 7:37-39, Psalm 36:8-9). He tells us to draw near to Him, ever poised to draw near to us (James 4:8). He says to seek Him with our whole heart, promising we will find Him (Jeremiah 29:12-13). He calls us to search out His hidden glory (Proverbs 25:2). He speaks His message to us in order that His joy would overflow in us, and we would enjoy Him to the fullest (John 15:11).

These are just a few examples of God's desire for us to know Him and experience Him abundantly. There are so many more.

I truly believe God wants us to encounter His immeasurable grace more and more. I believe He has wondrous things to show us from His riches!

Paul says in his letter to the Ephesians that the Father's heart in saving us was to put the immeasurable riches of His grace on full display for all to see, so that throughout time, "He might show the boundless riches of His grace in kindness toward us in Christ Jesus." (Ephesians 2:7, NASB).

The apostle Peter encourages us to "grow in the grace and the knowledge of our Lord and Savior, Jesus Christ" (2 Peter 3:18, NKJV).

Peter actually starts both of his letters with a blessing: for grace to be "multiplied" to his readers through the knowledge of God and of Jesus our Lord (1 Peter 1:2, 2 Peter 1:2).

This theme of abounding grace is echoed throughout the New Testament by other writers (John 1:16, James 4:6, 2 Corinthians 9:8).

And as stated before, the apostle Paul starts and ends his letters by speaking a blessing over his readers, that God's grace would be with them always.

In his letter to the Ephesians, Paul prays another beautiful prayer. In it, he prays for us to grow in our experiential knowledge of God. And while this particular prayer has to do more specifically with knowing and experiencing *the love of God* more intimately, and in greater measure; the principle remains the same: *God wants us to experience more.*

Furthermore, as we will see, God's grace and love go hand in hand. (2 Thessalonians 2:16, 1 Timothy 1:14, 2 Corinthians 13:14, etc).

Paul prays for us "to know the love of Christ which passes knowledge; that you may be filled with all the fullness of God." (Ephesians 3:19, NKJV)

In the New Living Translation, it reads: "May you experience the love of Christ, though it is too great to understand fully. Then you will be made complete with all the fullness of life and power that comes from God." (Ephesians 3:19, NLT)

I hope by now the vision for this book is coming to life.

The early apostles gave their lives for us to hear it and have it in abundance. They prayed for us to experience all of God in ever-increasing ways. Jesus Himself died so we could live in the absolute fullness of it.

God's grace – and further, God Himself – must be a treasure of immeasurable value, friend, which God and His servants want us to experience for ourselves.

So, we are embarking on an adventure: of mining the depths of Scripture for the priceless treasures hidden in this gospel of grace. We'll do so in a posture of prayer, with our hearts and arms wide open, full of faith and wonder.

Speaking of mining, let's explore one more illustration to help us in our journey.

The Scripture describes God's grace as "manifold" (1 Peter 4:10), meaning "many-sided."

The puritans would also describe the gospel as a multifaceted, or "many-sided" diamond.

A diamond's particular beauty manifests in how it interacts with light. You truly behold a diamond's glory when you hold it up in the light and begin to rotate it.

This is due to the intricate, masterful placement of various cuts, or "facets" on the jewel; and the resulting interchange and transfer of light between the facets.

When you turn a diamond in the light, even with the slightest rotation, you will observe a captivating dance of light. Jewelers have words to describe different elements of this.

Now, I'm no jeweler. I simply write from my own fascination and understanding – albeit rough and unpolished – that I have gathered from the mines of research. Here's my understanding:

First, there are the bright, radiant beams of pure white light that shine up and out through the diamond. This is referred to as the diamond's *"brilliance."* If the diamond cutter has done a quality job, there will be a compelling contrast of dark and light tones within the diamond, as well as a strong, striking return of light coming back out.

As it turns, radiant twirls of color will seem to spontaneously flash and break forth from within the diamond, like bursting rainbow pirouettes. The color is called the diamond's *"fire"* and it is caused by a diamond's facets dispersing pure white light into a spectrum of color. A similar effect can be observed after a rain shower or by shining light through a prism.

Finally, while the diamond is in motion, there is the way the beams of light seem to "dance" or "skip" or "flourish" from facet to facet, through the center of the diamond, appearing like shooting stars across the gem. This is referred to as the diamond's *"sparkle"* or pattern scintillation. This aspect is crucial, because most diamonds (on rings, for example) are not held still, but ever in motion.

These three work together in a complementary way, as in a dance, to unveil the beauty of a diamond in the light.

The more skillful the diamond cutter, the better the quality of the cuts, and the more intentionally and carefully the facets are aligned and prepared: the more fire, brilliance, and sparkle you will see in the diamond when the light strikes it.

This is why you will see people holding up their diamond rings in the light in awe, staring at them as they turn them delicately to admire them. They are looking for its fire, sparkle, and brilliance.

The gospel of grace is like that.

It gets better. See, God is the master diamond cutter. Every aspect of His grace was eternally planned out, and so carefully crafted; and each facet was so perfectly cut so as to play off the others.

And yes, there is a dynamic contrast of dark and light tones within the gospel story. But when we at last hold it up to the light, we watch in awe at how this all works together somehow, to return the light of God back out of it with stunning brilliance! What a miracle!

This is all designed to reveal the wonder of God within the gospel of Jesus Christ. We lift the diamond of the gospel up to God – who is Light – and we begin to turn it in the glow of His radiance. As we begin to admire its beauty from all the different angles, we behold:

The brilliance of the Father: eternally beaming His pure, strong, everlasting love from the core of the diamond!

The fire of the Holy Spirit: bursting forth in power throughout, in vivid, expressive technicolor!

The sparkle of the Son – Incarnate One, "God with us" – the Way between Heaven and earth: communicating the love, power and light of the gospel, and moving through all of it like a shooting star! Jesus Christ is the gospel of grace in motion!

I am sure the implications in this imagery could go on and on. The metaphor itself could be viewed from different angles!

And the truth is, the diamond of the gospel is far too intricate for any one book or sitting to cover. We will be observing its beauty for all eternity, catching new and thrilling flashes of light from an infinite number of angles.

But here's what I want to take away from all this.

Let us take time to admire the glorious gospel of grace.

In order to really appreciate the beauty of a diamond, *we must take our time with it.* We must hold it up in the light, and begin to turn it slowly.

That's what we will do here, friend. And it is in that spirit that I studied for and wrote this book.

In preparation, I searched the Scripture for the theme of grace.

I looked up the Greek and Hebrew words that get translated "grace" in English, and read through all of the scriptures where they appear, and their context. I read studies on the concept. I read cross-references and concordances. And I prayed a great deal.

As I searched, I began to see certain patterns emerge, and saw images fitting together like puzzle pieces. You could say these are aspects, or "facets" of God's grace.

Although, my particular arrangement is only one way to peer into the infinite beauty within the gospel. My prayer is that God would speak to you through His Word, above all else!

I wanted to pull from the loving devotion and rigorous work of Bible translators throughout time, to explore these facets more richly. So I have included Scripture from 20 different translations.

Some translations took a more word-for-word approach, some are more idea-for-idea. Some literal, some paraphrase. Some are newer works, some are more classic. Some are expanded, some direct and simple. I've tried to include a good balance of all these.

If you have a "go-to" translation, I encourage you to follow along side-by-side with that one! Make the journey your own!

There may be times where words or phrases are repeated a lot, but that's also the point. Sort of like the melodic theme showing up in different variations throughout the symphony. It may be on the fifteenth repetition of the melody, now presented in a romantic waltz variation, that your heart is struck by glory and your eyes well up with tears of joy.

Our goal is to look at grace richly from its many sides – in essence, to "turn the diamond" in the light – and to really take our time with it.

As we rotate the gospel of grace, and look intently at it from different angles: new joys and revelations sparkle and burst forth in the light of God, and we grow in our appreciation for the beauty of *both* the diamond *and* the light!

My goal was to cast a vision and set a context for our adventure ahead, before embarking. Now that we have that, let's talk about how we'll go about it.

6

HOW TO USE THIS BOOK: PREPARING FOR THE JOURNEY

I told you that I wrote the book I would have wanted.

You can use it any way you'd like, really. But for anyone who would want them, here are a few thoughts and ideas I've gathered from my own personal experience that might enrich your time.

If we are about to embark on a treasure hunt, the next few chapters are like an equipment room. My hope is that in them, we can pick up a few things like headlamps, compasses, a treasure map, a couple shovels, some solid boots, and a sturdy bag to put it all in.

Maybe God will even load us up with a really high-tech metal detector, that lights up when glorious treasure is nearby. And perhaps, He has already given us tools just like this, and we are discovering that we have them, and how to use them!

Well, with that said ...

TAKING OUR TIME

You may notice that there are 31 chapters in Part Two. Originally, this was going to be a 1-month devotional, but it kept opening up and expanding. You can certainly still use it that way, if you are inspired to.

My first and main encouragement, if you'd like it, would be to really *soak it all in:* really leaving space and time to be drawn in, to savor the glorious word of grace.

One way to go about this, is simply to ask the Holy Spirit to speak to you and encounter you as you go, and remove any pressure to read this at any pace. God often speaks to us in the stillness, in ways that can surprise us, when we let go of preconceived ideas and simply engage God with a listening heart.

In the famous words of Mother Teresa, "God speaks in the silence of the heart. Listening is the beginning of prayer."

Really turn the diamond slowly, and let it sparkle in the light. And if something catches your eye, feel free to stay right there! Meditate on that facet, and really let its beauty sink in; even if it means stopping in the middle of a chapter, putting down the book, and picking up at that spot another time.

Perhaps, in one instance, your reading of this book might end up revolving around just one scripture. That's perfectly great. If it leads you to experiencing God and His grace in any way, then the purpose of this book was accomplished!

As stated before, the intention of this book is that you would experience God and His grace through Scripture and prayer.

So, on that note, here's one thing to try.

HEARING THE WORD OF GRACE

Read the verses, with the prayerful expectation that *God wants to meet with you* in them. If you want, you can read them out loud. Really hear the words as you say them, or in your heart if you are reading silently.

Listen intently. Really hear.

Is there a word that seems to stand out? A phrase, or idea? Maybe it's the word "love," or the phrase, "grace upon grace," or a picture of Jesus giving his life on the Cross.

Consider this: What if this is standing out to you in this moment because God is wanting to show you something?

Let's just entertain the thought that this is exactly what is happening. With that context, meditate on that word, phrase, or idea. Turn it around slowly in your heart. You might even repeat it out loud. If it helps to focus, you could close your eyes.

With this portion in mind that stood out to you, you could ask God things like, "What do You want to say to me, God? How are You wanting to apply this to my life? What are You showing me about Yourself?" That kind of thing. Talk with God about it.

And perhaps, there in the stillness of the heart, see if things come to your awareness. Or even a sense of peace, hope, or joy. Or maybe a desire to keep reading further.

And as you hear, *receive*. Let God fill your heart.

These are all ways that God can encounter us through the word of grace. This is part of how faith can come by hearing, and hearing by the Word of God.

That's just one idea.

CRAFTING PRAYERS FROM THE SCRIPTURE

Then there are the written prayers. Let me expound on how I went about crafting those.

One thing I have loved to do when reading the Scripture, is to see what it says is true, personalize it for myself, and speak it out loud.

Maybe you have seen people craft "declarations" or "affirmations" from Scripture. My wife and I have had papers like this printed out around our different houses through the years. Sometimes, we'd just pick them up and start speaking them out loud. "I am a new creation in Christ! I am a beloved son of God!" And so on. I really love those.

I found what really magnified this experience – and what caused me to be deeply rooted and grounded in the grace, love and truth of Christ – was the added element of making it a *prayer*, almost like a conversation with God.

In turning my Bible reading into a prayer, I would actively engage with God and the words He breathed, echoing His own music back to Him. It transformed my awareness. I began to hear His symphony more throughout life, all around me and within me.

Let's say I set out to read in Ephesians, for instance. I would ask the Holy Spirit to speak to me through it, and I would embark. Then, I would come across something like this:

> Blessed be the God and Father of our Lord Jesus Christ, who has blessed us with every spiritual blessing in the heavenly places in Christ. *(Ephesians 1:3, NKJV)*

The metal detector would start going off. Treasure was in here.

What a rich collection of words, in just one verse!

I'd pause from my reading and be still. Maybe I'd repeat the reading. I would allow my heart to "hear" the words, and fill up with their grace and truth. Then, from the fullness of my heart, I'd turn my attention to speak to God, taking what I had read and turning it into prayer:

"My God, My Father! You are truly filled with blessing! Jesus, You are Lord, the Chosen One! I am humbled and amazed, Father, that I have been welcomed into God's family *forever*, as Your beloved son. It fills me with so much joy. Thank You, Father, for placing me In Christ. It says here, Jesus, that in You, I am blessed with every spiritual blessing in the Heavenly places. Wow, God, this is so amazing! Holy Spirit, I am asking You to show me the truth of what this all *really* means. I want to know You and Your grace more."

Something like that. It was spontaneous, and I grew in it the more I did it. I read through the Bible slower, but the time was so rewarding.

In writing this book, I gathered groups of scriptures that seemed to fit together. And then, I began to see the prayers form and fit together like a puzzle, as well. And I wrote prayers in the fashion I just described.

When it comes to God's grace, I continued to see a pattern emerge. So many of these scriptures declare what God has already done for us in Christ, or what He's already given us, or who He has always been: how His love is unfailing, and His grace abundant.

As this truth filled me, and I went to pray, the pattern went something like, "God, I worship You for who You are, and thank You for all You have done and all You have given! I pray to know more of You, and become more aware of all that is already ours in Christ, so that I can walk in Your life more fully!"

My goal has been to craft these prayers from Scripture, while listening for the Holy Spirit, and praying from the overflow of my heart.

With that said, use these prayers how you'd like.

Read the prayers out loud to God, or in your heart. And feel free to pause and reflect if something catches your attention.

Or craft your own prayers from what you hear God speak through the Scripture. Let it be like a conversation. Let Him speak through His Word, and as you listen, let it fill your heart. Then from the fullness of your heart, pray. Then God listens. Then do it all again. This is a wonderful way to pray.

Whether using these prayers or crafting your own, *pray from your heart,* and really speak to God. And as you pray, *believe* ...

This is part of what it means to "receive grace by faith."

In the next chapter, we will explore this concept a bit together, in hopes it can help equip us for the journey ahead.

7

RECEIVING GRACE BY FAITH

The gospel. The glad tidings. The Good News. The message of what Christ has done. The glorious word of grace.

Grace, wondrous grace.

Oh, Father, thank You for the people who have given their lives to *"the work of telling others the Good News about the wonderful grace of God."* (Acts 20:24, NLT).

How fortunate we are to be ones who have heard. What a gift it is to participate!

Let's pack a few more tools for our treasure hunt, friend, and search the Scripture for the wonderful grace of God. The following are concepts that have helped me do just that.

COME AND SEE WHAT GOD HAS DONE

Okay. Remember how I told you about different narrators and preachers we'd listen to through the years, and in the NICU?

And remember that trip we took to Colorado with our Judah?

So, we got to attend this powerful healing conference during our time in Colorado. I'll never forget it. When we were there, we got to meet one of our favorite preachers, whose voice tremendously encouraged us in the word of grace. He was the kindest person, full of grace and truth, much like the One he represents; the One living in him.

Greatest of all, we got to see God powerfully at work there. It was so amazing. We saw miraculous things happening right before our eyes!

Anyway, here's what I love. The gospel of grace was the foundation of the entire thing. It was all about magnifying what God has done, and relying on His grace, "so that in all things God may be glorified through Jesus Christ, to whom be the glory and the power forever and ever." (1 Peter 4:11, BSB).

We heard the same Good News of Jesus Christ there at that conference, that we heard in our headphones at the NICU, and that we read in our Bibles, and have heard passed down through the fathers and mothers of the faith ... all bearing witness, and saying in harmony:

> Come and see what God has done,
>
> his awesome deeds for mankind! *(Psalm 66:5, NIV)*
>
> ... the amazing [majestic] things he has done for people. *(EXB)*

We heard about *what God has done*. The amazing and majestic things He has done for people, and His awesome deeds for mankind. This is the word of grace, and we saw how God "was testifying to the word of His grace" with His miraculous power (Acts 14:3).

And I found that the more I would hear about *what God has done*, from testimonies people told, to the actual gospel preached from Scripture, the more I became aware of faith rising inside me. I believe we can never hear the gospel enough. I need the gospel every day ... *every moment.*

And what a rich time of hearing it was. We heard the Good News about how God already provided everything for life and godliness through the grace of Jesus Christ and His atoning sacrifice on the Cross, *once for all.* (2 Peter 1:3, 1 Peter 2:24, 1 Peter 3:18, Isaiah 53:5-6, Hebrews 10:10-14).

We heard the echo of Scripture, imploring us to believe and take hold of this for ourselves. This is our part: faith. We access by faith what God has already provided in the grace of Jesus Christ (Romans 5:2, Philemon 1:6, Ephesians 1:3, Ephesians 2:8-9).

God's promises, and His good news, become *reality* for us when we mix it with our faith. By faith, *we enter into God's rest,* "resting" in what He has already done. (Hebrews 4:1-3).

This is certainly not a new idea. I believe it's scriptural, first and foremost. And, many have committed their lives to glorifying God by testifying to His grace revealed in Scripture. This is a timeless message. As it is written:

> ... This grace was given us in Christ Jesus before the beginning of time, but it has now been revealed through the appearing of our Savior, Christ Jesus, who has destroyed death and has brought life and immortality to light through the gospel. *(1 Timothy 1:9-10, NIV)*

The apostles were the first to spread the "Good News" of the grace revealed through Jesus Christ. In the voices of Peter, John, and Paul ... You can hear the true fulfillment of Psalm 66:5 resounding in the message they carried: *"Come and see what God has done!"*

Since then, many others have glorified God by speaking His Word, delivering the gospel, sharing what He has already done through Christ and His "finished work" (John 19:30).

Martin Luther (1483–1546), often called the "Father of the Reformation," was renowned for his revelation of grace, and echoed this theme in his writings:

> Grace says, "Believe in this," and everything is already done.[1]

In this same vein, Charles Spurgeon (1834–1892), often called the "Prince of Preachers," spoke of resting in the finished work of Jesus Christ:

> Now let us find solace in the finished work of our Lord Jesus. Everything is fully done: justice demands no more.[2]

Grace means God has given. Everything is fully done. Our part is to receive it.

What a tremendous revelation.

I mentioned my dear mentor and friend, D. W. Martin, in my opening dedication of this book. He's been like a spiritual father to me, especially in this word of grace. We all call him Dwayne.

In his powerful book, *Grace Whisperers*, Dwayne expounds at length on this concept of receiving grace by faith. In it he says:

> When we receive God, He provides the power and we rest.[3]

Wow. God provides the power. We receive. We rest.

FAITH COMES BY HEARING

How? Simply: we receive by faith.

And "faith comes by hearing, and hearing by the Word of God" (Romans 10:17, NKJV). Or "hearing the Good News about Christ" (NLT).

Let's reflect on this verse from Romans for a moment. Here is some beauty I see, sparkling in this word.

As we embark on our journey of reading through Scripture, and asking Holy Spirit to speak to us through it, this verse helps me to realize something powerful:

Whenever the Word of the Lord comes to us, when we "hear the Good News" ... God has also made sure that the *ability to believe* and *receive His Word* is present with us the moment that we hear it.

In short: We always have all we need to receive the word of grace by faith.

This is great news. The table is set already.

Here's an illustration you might find helpful.

Imagine a treasure chest that comes with the key needed to open it. The treasure chest is the Word, the treasure inside is grace, the key is faith.

Wherever the message is, faith is also available.

The Good News of Christ could also be seen like a magnet to faith, causing it to stir and rise as it comes near.

Here's what I see: faith rises in us when we *hear* the Word of God, the glad message of Christ and all He has done, the glorious gospel of grace ... And blessed are they who hear *and keep hearing* the Good News, over and over ...

And by "hear," I don't believe this necessarily means audibly, since someone could "hear" the Good News from reading. What I do believe may be important here, is that we are *actively listening* for His Word *with our hearts open*.

Although, let me glorify God ... I think His Word often miraculously pierces through the most closed hearts. And I believe God can soften hearts (Ezekiel 36:26), and give us eyes to see and ears to hear (Proverbs 20:12). And He can show us how to remove any obstructions in our hearts and lives that would hinder His Word from taking deep root in us (Matthew 13:1-23).

We can ask Him for all these things in prayer, for ourselves and even others. Isn't God endlessly kind?

That said, I believe that there is something important here about opening our hearts to God, taking a humble posture of listening ... leaning in expectantly to really hear Him ... and receiving His Word with joy, accepting it for what it really is: not the word of people, but *the Word of God*:

> For this reason we also constantly thank God that when you received the word of God which you heard from us, you accepted *it* not *as* the word of *mere* men, but as what it really is, the word of God, which also is at work in you who believe. *(1 Thessalonians 2:13, NASB)*

When we welcome the Word of God with this due reverence, it goes to work in us, and continues to work in us, effectively and powerfully:

> ... you welcomed it not as the word of [mere] men, but as it truly is, the word of God, which is effectually at work in you who believe [exercising its inherent, supernatural power in those of faith]. *(1 Thessalonians 2:13, AMP)*

> ... [exercising its superhuman power in those who adhere to and trust in and rely on it]. *(AMPC)*

Wow. May we hear the glorious Good News of the grace of Christ, and welcome it with open hearts as the very Word of God! May we trust in and rely on it, that it may exercise its inherent, supernatural, *superhuman* power within us!

And let us remember this wonderful truth: wherever the message is, faith is also available. The treasure chest comes with the key.

See, the message activates faith in our lives. And then in turn, *faith* activates the *message* in our lives. Isn't this amazing?

I find it helpful to acknowledge two important things which seem to be held in balance here.

First: God has created and provided everything necessary for this whole process. We have it because God supplies it. Thank You, God!

Second: That being said, we also still have an important, necessary and active role to play. Our part is to *respond to Him*, by *acting in faith*.

Grace is God's part, faith is our part. God's free gift, and our response. This is the balance.

Like two substances that create a chemical reaction: when God's grace and our faith mix in balance, we see something spectacular happen before our eyes. We see Heaven come to earth.

Faith becomes alive when we take action. This is, at first, to "turn the key" and open the treasure chest, by praying in agreement with Scripture, as we will do in this book.

And then, to "make use of" the gifts inside, by doing the things that faith would have us do, living life from the truth of that Word. By this, we become hearers and doers of the word, and are truly blessed and happy (James 1:22-25). As Jesus said,

> "... blessed *are* those who hear the word of God and keep it!" *(Luke 11:28, NKJV).*

We hear the Word, believe it and receive it by faith in prayer. It works its supernatural power within us.

And then we "keep" it, living from its truth: living as if we have truly received what's inside of it, and God has given the power and supply to back up everything the Word says. Because, as it is written:

"You have observed correctly," said the LORD, "for I am watching over My word to accomplish it." *(Jeremiah 1:12, BSB)*

"You have seen well, for I am [actively] watching over My word to fulfill it." *(AMP)*

"... until it is fulfilled." *(CEB)*

He is actively watching over His Word to fulfill it, until it is fulfilled. And in Christ – from Heaven's side – *it already is* fulfilled. *That which is true in Heaven* fills the earth through us acting in faith, from the abundance of His grace.

God provides the power, and we rest in Him.

Let's again return to the words of my mentor, Dwayne:

When we receive God, He provides the power and we rest.

Let's meet God in His message, and *receive Him for ourselves*. Let's receive His glorious grace by faith, and enter His rest.

As it says in Hebrews,

Let's make every effort to enter into that rest. *(Hebrews 4:11, NASB)*

"Make every effort"? Hm. This must be very important. So let's go a little further with this. Let us hear the Word of Christ, mix it with our faith, and *enter into the rest of God.*

ENTERING INTO GOD'S REST

This passage in Hebrews 4 reveals something beautiful: this act of "receiving God's grace by faith" actually reflects *the original "day of rest."*

Think back to the creation of the world, and the moment when God made the very first human beings in His image. In the first six days, God had already masterfully created and provided everything in the universe. Then, in creation's grand finale, God at last breathed the breath of life into the first humans, and *they opened their eyes to a world already made.*

They were born into God's abundance. And God welcomes them with a blessing: to receive, live in, and explore His already finished work. Yes, they had important things to do. God put them in charge, telling them to fill the earth and govern it, and to steward what He had given. But it was all action to be taken *from abundance*, and *from rest*.

After blessing His crowning creation, the very next thing God did was, "God looked upon all that He had made, and indeed, it was very good ... Thus the heavens and the earth were completed in all their vast array." (Genesis 1:31-2:1, BSB). They were born into completion. This ends the sixth day.

And on the seventh day, God rested from His work, because creation was complete. Do you know what this means? It means humanity's entire first new day of existence was all about one thing: *entering into God's rest*. They rested with God, enjoying all He had already done. Their purpose was to look upon all His work and say in agreement: "It is very good!" God *blessed* this day, and *declared it holy*.

Now Christ is called the "Last Adam" and the "Second Man", which points us to a new creation, a new birth, and a new world.

So too, when we are born again and created anew in Christ, we enter into God's rest. We receive the Holy Spirit as the breath of new life, and we first open our eyes to a wondrous new creation *already complete*, to explore a work *already finished*. We are born into abundance. We are born into completion.

Just as they began new life by waking up to the seventh day in Eden, our new life in Christ begins by awakening to God's Heavenly reality, and glorifying our God, who has already done it all on our behalf.

> For all who have entered into God's rest have rested from their labors, just as God did after creating the world. *(Hebrews 4:10, NLT)*

This is all so amazing. God has done it. Jesus our High Priest *sat down* on the throne. And we rest in Him. Faith begins by agreeing with God: "Father, Your work is complete, and it is *very good*." This is blessed. *This is holy*.

And yes, we absolutely have important things to do. Dominion to take, and grace to steward. We make *every effort* to enter into this rest, taking hold of what is already true in the new creation. This is the "grace in which we stand" that we access and receive by faith through Christ (Romans 5:2).

We do not want to fall short of grace, by unbelief. No, we want to continually cling to the word of grace, working out our salvation. And approach the throne of grace to find help in time of need. This is all a part of our journey in this world! But let us remember, *we are not of this world.* (John 17:11)

And it all starts by acknowledging our new birth, and the grace of God. In His eyes, we find the truth of our identity. With unveiled face, we behold God's glory *as in a mirror*, and the Spirit transforms us into His image, from glory to glory (2 Corinthians 3:18).

We have been eternally born again in Christ (1 Peter 1:23), in the very likeness of God (Ephesians 4:24), as citizens of Heaven (Philippians 3:20). A new creation in a new world. The old has gone. Behold, *everything is new.* (2 Corinthians 5:17).

They were placed in the garden in Eden. We have been placed in Christ.

And now, we get to live *from God's abundance* in the Spirit, and go forth *from His rest*. We get to enjoy what Christ has done, and live in our Father's Kingdom as good stewards of God's grace. We get to fill the earth with the very life of God, which is springing forth *inside of us* like the rivers in Eden (John 7:38-39).

Wow. Holy, holy, holy.

What does this mean for our journey ahead?

We have an infinite garden of glorious grace to explore.

Okay. So, let's repeat some simple truths.

We receive grace by faith. Faith is fully present with us the moment we hear the Word of God. And we exercise this faith of ours by praying, and *believing* as we pray; and receiving God for ourselves.

Once again: *We have all we need to receive God's grace by faith in Christ.*

This is like Adam and Eve eating from the Tree of Life. We have been given access to the life of God, to partake of it freely. Our part is to take the fruit and eat.

Reading, "hearing" and praying the word of grace – as we'll do in this book – is one way this all comes together, in brilliant, living color. In doing so, we "take hold" of the grace God has already made available to us through Christ. *"On earth as it is in Heaven."*

See, in praying this way, we will be doing what Dwayne would repeatedly exhort me to do: to "take hold of that for which Christ Jesus took hold of me." (Philippians 3:12, NIV). We pray as Jesus taught us, "having faith in God," and "believing we have received" what we prayed, and "it will be ours." (Mark 11:24, BSB).

And we enter into His rest. We partake of God's life. Grace becomes truly ours.

I have taken time to really orbit around this idea, so we are abundantly ready to partake in the life of God.

So once more, let us declare our purpose:

We read and really listen. We believe and sincerely pray. We receive and fully enjoy.

And from this place, we take action and live in newness of life.

This is truly exciting to take hold of. This is sharing in the very life of Christ.

Dwayne continues in his book:

> Faith tells us all we need to do is receive and confess the grace of God, our new given birthright ...[4]

I want to mention Martin Luther again. He was one who did this. A pioneer of grace. He saw and heard the grace of God. He believed it. And he received it for himself, as his new birthright in Christ.

In fact, he was so enraptured and compelled by the word of grace, that he staked his very life on it. He wrote:

> Faith is a living, daring confidence in God's grace, so sure and certain that a man would stake his life on it one thousand times. This confidence in God's grace and knowledge of it makes men glad and bold and happy in dealing with God and with all creatures; and this is the work of the Holy Ghost in faith.[5]

Oh the happiness of the one who receives the grace of God, freely given through Christ!

Can you hear it in Luther's words, as he speaks of the life, joy and boldness that comes from confidently believing in the grace of God? Do you see the power of the Holy Spirit at work within him as he places all his trust in God's grace? What wonders he must have witnessed as he opened the Scripture!

This is our aim: to encounter those same wonders for ourselves, as we read and pray the word of grace. We have the same Holy Spirit, and the same access. May we enter by faith into the divine rest of God and His glorious grace!

As we hear Luther's statement, and listen to what Christ and His followers say in Scripture, and as we look at their actions, we see that truly: "God's rest" is not one that dulls or slows us. It is a rest that *invigorates us, frees us,* and *empowers us.*

And we are *reinvigorated* every time we experience the gospel of grace *afresh.*

SEEING WITH FRESH EYES

The Bible verses in this book contain statements that are absolutely life-altering if we really sit with them, and open our hearts to them. This is why I suggest taking our time. God's grace is breathtakingly wonderful, and the implications of the finished work of Christ are staggering.

Believe it or not, I actually edited at least 200 exclamation points out of the first draft of the written prayers, so as to not sound like I was shouting the whole time. Ha! I didn't even realize I was typing all of them. I guess I just got carried away and found it difficult not to emphasize every statement, because it was all just so glorious!!!!!

You know, I have noticed that many times, I have skimmed over these amazing claims, as I would hurry through a Bible reading. Or perhaps I had become familiar with certain ideas through repeated liturgy or lingo. Maybe you can relate to this.

Well, my encouragement is for us to listen with fresh ears, and look with fresh eyes. Pray like you are finding out for the very first time.

Or, if you like, pray like you're seeing a beautiful brand new flower bloom right before your eyes, in a garden you are very at home in, and very fond of already. Come with the wonder of a child.

When I've done this, even for 30 seconds, it has been so life-giving.

By its very definition, something being "infinite" means you cannot reach the end of it. There are always new facets, layers, and revelations of God's glory and grace to experience.

Let faith rise up as you hear the message of Christ, and then *exercise* that faith as you pray and speak. When we really let the melody of grace resonate in our hearts, it's as though our very soul is expanded with new life. It's so thrilling!

Here's an example of what I mean. Let's read these familiar words of Peter, who is declaring how Jesus has at last fulfilled the prophetic words of Isaiah, saying to us:

> By His wounds we have been healed. *(1 Peter 2:24, CSB)*

Wow ... Let's pause and reflect on that for a moment.

What do these words *truly mean?* By the wounds of Jesus, *we have been healed!*

Let's sit with this verse, and let's *really hear it ...*

Let's really entertain the thought: what if this is true? What if I fully accepted this? What are the implications of that for me, and my whole life? Right here, right now, right where I am ...

Let's allow God to fill our hearts with this awesome, life-transforming word. Let's open our eyes wide to the bright new creation in Christ, and enter into the rest of what God has done.

And as we read this verse, let's watch for the life and presence of the Holy Spirit. Let's listen for grace. What part is jumping out at us: Wounds? Have been? Healed? His? We?

Ruminate on it ... turn it in the light ... watch it sparkle.

Just seven words, yet so many powerful ways the Holy Spirit can move within them. There is infinite glory here.

Hopefully, all of these concepts are beginning to come together.

And as we press on together, let's keep asking God to show us His glory. He is faithful! Let's ask Him to reveal the depths of His glorious riches in every verse that we read, and every prayer that we pray.

His radiant light is already shining brilliantly, and the diamond of the gospel of grace is already masterfully cut. Let's ask Him to position our hearts to see its beauty from another angle, and give us ears to hear and eyes to see. Let's ask that He open our eyes afresh to His finished work, that we may believe and enter into His rest.

He will always give us wisdom when we ask:

> If any of you lacks wisdom, you should ask God, who gives generously to all without finding fault, and it will be given to you. *(James 1:5, NIV)*

He gives generously because it's who He is! He is the ultimate giver. We simply must ask in faith that He will answer.

In fact, let's believe that He *loves to answer.*

JOYFUL EXPECTATION

I told you we posted scriptures all over our unit at the NICU. There was one other phrase we had posted up, and even had printed on T-Shirts.

We heard this story while in the NICU. A famous owner of a basketball team would tell the players before every game to go into it with this mindset: "Expect to win."

The phrase caught on with us at the NICU. We would whisper it to each other all the time, as we looked at the days ahead of us: *expect to win.* For us, it was a reminder to keep our stance grounded firmly in the *victory that Christ has already won on our behalf.*

Here's my encouragement: let's read and pray *with expectation.*

Go through these scriptures and prayers with the expectation of encountering God. Open your heart to every word being actual reality.

Pray with the expectation that – as you are praying – you are actually, *genuinely* reaching into the abundance of Heaven's resources, and drawing out buckets full of glory from the wells of His grace. Posture your heart for a breakthrough of God's amazing grace, coming right around the corner. Expect to win.

The Greek word for "hope" in Scripture is defined as a "joyful expectation." And in the letter to the Romans, this blessing is spoken over us:

> May the God of hope fill you with all joy and peace as you trust in him, so that you may overflow with hope by the power of the Holy Spirit. *(Romans 15:13, NIV)*

So, in this overflow of hope, by the power of the Holy Spirit: let us go forward in the *joyful expectation* that *God wants to* open "the eyes of our understanding" (Ephesians 1:18, NKJV). It's what He does. It's who He is!

Consider this as a prophetic picture from the Gospel of Matthew:

> Then He touched their eyes, saying, "According to your faith let it be to you." And their eyes were opened ... *(Matthew 9:29-30, NKJV)*

Let's come to Him, in the confidence that He is able and willing to touch our eyes, and open them to the wondrous mysteries of His grace, *so that we may see. This is what our God does.*

In the words of the prophet Daniel:

> But there is a God in heaven who reveals mysteries ... *(Daniel 2:28, HCSB)*

This is our God, who said through His Son Jesus:

> Ask and it will be given to you; seek and you will find; knock and the door will be opened to you. For everyone who asks receives; the one who seeks finds; and to the one who knocks, the door will be opened. *(Matthew 7:7-8, NIV)*

Jesus reveals that this is who our God is: *a good Father*, who gives good gifts to those who ask Him (Matthew 7:9-11, James 1:17).

> And He has made known to us the mystery of His will according to His good pleasure, which He purposed in Christ *(Ephesians 1:9, BSB)*

It is *our Father's good pleasure* to make His heart known to us, to give us wisdom from above (James 1:5). It is *our Father's good pleasure* to give us the kingdom (Luke 12:32). He wants us to receive, and *He wants us to see.*

He loves to reveal Himself to us, and reveal Heaven's mysteries to us. And He is found by those who sincerely seek him, with the simple trust, openness and wonder of a little child. (Proverbs 25:2, 1 Corinthians 2:10, Colossians 1:26, Jeremiah 29:13, Jeremiah 33:3, Exodus 33:18-19, John 1:14, Matthew 21:22, Hebrews 11:6, Luke 10:21).

And as we trust in Him, the God of all hope fills us with all joy and peace, til we overflow! (Romans 15:13).

God has given us access to all the hidden treasures of grace in Christ. Let us hold the precious Scripture like a treasure map, and allow the Holy Spirit to be our compass and guiding voice. Let us seek, with the expectation that *we will find!*

Let us pray with this joyful expectation: *God wants us to hear His heart and receive His grace.*

In fact, the Lord *longs to be gracious to us.*

> Yet the LORD longs to be gracious to you; therefore he will rise up to show you compassion. *(Isaiah 30:18, NIV)*

I believe that God is waiting, longing to share His love and abundant life with us (John 10:10). He has prepared the table of grace for us (Psalm 23:5). He has remarkable secrets to share with us (Jeremiah 33:3, NLT). His heart is calling ours with an invitation to meet with us intimately, and share a meal with us as dear friends (Revelation 3:20, NLT).

Can you hear the heartbeat of the Father?

He's the kind of Father who comes running down the road to meet us. He throws feasts for His beloved children, showers them with His affection, and tells them, "everything I have is yours." (Luke 15:31, NIV).

This is our Father. *He is such a good Father.*

He satisfies the longing soul,

And fills the hungry soul with goodness. *(Psalm 107:9, NKJV)*

Oh dear friend ... let's respond to His lavish heart. Let's open our arms wide to welcome the Word of Life, and receive His glorious grace by faith!

Wonderful Father, we come with ready hearts to the table of grace, the feast of Your goodness, longing to meet with You, and expecting You with great joy, saying:

My soul shall be satisfied as with the richest food.

My mouth shall praise you with joyful lips. *(Psalm 63:5, NHEB)*

Amen!

8

FAITHFULLY WRESTLING

And yet ...

Perhaps you still struggle to trust in the wondrous things written in the word of grace.

I have certainly been there. In this chapter, we'll explore what it might mean to engage with these words in the midst of painful dissonance in our hearts.

Before I go on ... I know I must sound like a broken record here, yet again saying "this topic is a whole other book" ...

However, I do want take the time to admit to the inherent limitations of briefly touching on deep matters. I am aware that this book on prayer cannot truly treat certain subjects with all the gravity they deserve; theologically, emotionally or otherwise.

For instance, consider this subject of faithfully wrestling through the tension held between the wounds of our history and the truth claims of Scripture. There is so much that could be said about both sides of that tension.

So I am praying for the grace to write here, knowing the picture will be incomplete, and I am asking for God to speak His perfect love through human imperfections. I also ask you for forgiveness, for the nuances I won't be able to touch on here.

With those limitations in mind, I felt like expounding on this topic a little more, and describing what has helped me as I've engaged with Scripture in moments that felt incredibly dark, and too much to bear.

These were also the moments where I would ultimately find the Light that heals, and the Love that bears all things ...

My prayer is that this could help someone, and better establish another tool for the journey ahead.

So let me say it once more.

Perhaps you still struggle to trust in the wondrous things written about in the word of grace.

I understand that struggle, friend, though I will absolutely *admit* and *respect* that I am unable to fully understand your unique life story.

Far more importantly, though, I believe that Jesus *intimately* knows and understands, empathizes and cares (Hebrews 4:14-16). He was "a man of sorrows, acquainted with deepest grief" (Isaiah 53:3). He has clothed Himself with our humanity (John 1:14).

And, He has grace for the struggle, *in abundance.* For, this same Jesus who died our death, is now risen in glory, seated on His Heavenly throne, *on our behalf.* We can approach His throne of grace *with confidence* in our time of need: freely, boldly and without reservation (Hebrews 4:14-16). He *gives more grace,* wherever we need help (James 4:6). We only need to ask.

Remember the stories I told you, about the internal tension my wife and I felt as we encountered the message of God's goodness after the death of our son? Like the moment we heard that beautiful worship song, and it hit a painful nerve in a tired soul.

Remember the struggling father who brought his son to Jesus for deliverance? *"I believe; help my unbelief!"* (Mark 9:24, ESV)

I have found myself in that tug of war, between what the gospel says is true, and the pain in my heart and its resulting interpretation of the world around me. Between the invisible and the visible. In the tension of Heaven and earth.

Well, here is another thing you could do with this book: *wrestle with it faithfully.* You could pray through it with an open and honest heart, like David prayed in his Psalms. Let these pages lead you into vulnerable processing ...

"God, I hear this and I am scared to believe it. I feel hurt here. I feel tired. But I want so badly to believe it. Are You really this faithful? Speak to me, Holy Spirit. Help my unbelief. Come into this place in my heart, and dwell there with Your healing light. I am open to You."

That's just an example. Probably even a mild one. However it sounds to you, I encourage you to let Him into those places.

Honestly, sometimes I had no words, only tears. Or screams. Or burdened sighs. Sometimes it was really loud, and really messy. Sometimes it was so quiet, and I barely had a groan of anxious desperation. Whatever I had, I poured it all out at the foot of the Cross, and asked God to come in.

And I believe He always answered that prayer, filling that space *with Himself.*

In this journey of faithful wrestling, I really began to ask the question: "What if He wants to connect with me right here, *in this* place?" Not looking at it from a distance, but inside of it. Just like when God *entered in* and became a flesh-and-blood human being (John 1:14) ...

Just like what God did with me that day in my car, at my son's graveside ...

If you need proof of His intention, just look at Jesus. His death on the Cross. His birth in an animal trough. From the first day to the last of His earthly ministry, He showed that He is not afraid of messy, dirty, ugly, dark or scary.

In fact, I would submit He came to seek and save us, to find us and to love us, in those very places. We need only to let Him in, and receive Him. He embraces us right in the middle of the mess. He hears our hearts. He understands us. We all need grace, and He gave it to all: there is no one too far from its reach.

Grace is the love of God that reaches down, goes to our deepest depths, and meets us in our own world, no matter how dark it may seem. He loves us ... *completely and without reservation.*

Oh, how He loves us ...

And then, grace *lifts us up.* He comes into the darkness, and He shines His light. He brings us home. Wherever Christ abides, He fills the space with peace, joy, and love. That which He inhabits, He heals, He restores, He renews, He resurrects ... *He ascends ...*

And oh, how He loves us ...

Here, we are beginning to see a completion of this idea of "faithfully wrestling" with Scripture. We ask: what is the fullness of this process, where do we leave off with it?

It begins with us letting Him into the darkness. It completes with Him shining His light.

Somehow, it's both. Fully. The honesty of earth meets the truth of Heaven. The cross and the resurrection. This is the completion.

And I have found the order to be key: earth is the question. Heaven is the answer.

Jesus, the Word of God, is the answer.

I have brought a lot of raw feelings to the Lord, that felt incredibly real and valid. And I always found compassion, and understanding in that place. The complete acceptance and warm embrace of a loving Father.

And ... there was much more.

A completion came in going forward in the strength of His love and grace ... and in circling back around to the truth of Scripture, and planting my faith there.

In other words: when establishing what I believe, I chose to focus on what He says is true, over and above any feelings I was experiencing.

First, I would open my heart in total honesty in His presence, accepting this is simply where I'm at in this moment. Then, I would invite God into that place.

Then at some point, I would find myself returning to what He says. I would rely and lean on His grace and truth to lead me; to remind me of who He is, and who I am in Him.

Though we may *feel* beaten, this is truly an act of faith, to say:

> Return to your rest, my soul, for the Lord has been good to you. *(Psalm 116:7, NIV)*

Oh, the stories I could tell you ... the moments when death surrounded me, and I fell to my knees ... and then I lifted my head to sing of the God who brings life ...

And oh, how the atmosphere changes when we remember the goodness of our God.

Let's look at one of the Psalms.

Psalm 42 represents an honest prayer coming from a discouraged believer. Some say it was written by David. Some attribute it to the Sons of Korah. Since I don't have the knowledge there, I will just refer to its writer as "the psalmist."

Here, the psalmist begins by speaking of the desperate state that his soul is in. He is crying out for God, longing for His presence. He pours out his hurt before the Lord:

> My tears have been my food day and night,
>
> While they say to me all day long, "Where is your God?" *(Psalm 42:3, AMP)*

He then remembers the days when he would lead congregations in worship (Psalm 42:4). Glorious days, filled with joy and thanksgiving.

However, at the time of writing this, he feels dry, cast out and alone. On top of that, others now seem to be mocking him for his belief in God. He gets brutally honest about what he feels:

> O my God, my soul is in despair within me [the burden more than I can bear] ... *(Psalm 42:6, AMP)*

The burden is more than he can bear ... And yet, in the midst of all this pain, he continually brings his focus back to God and His truth.

> ... Therefore I will [fervently] remember You from the land of the Jordan ... *(Psalm 42:6, AMP)*

He takes time to remember all the good things God has done — *fervently and on purpose* — to encourage himself in the Lord. This is the remedy. He repeats: *"Yet I will praise Him again."*

Several times, the psalmist even speaks to his own heart, as if it is an entity distinct from himself. It sounds to me almost as though he is speaking to his soul like a precious, scared child. One whom he is comforting, gently teaching, and leading into God's loving arms.

> Why are you in despair, O my soul?
>
> Why have you become restless and disquieted within me?
>
> Hope in God and wait expectantly for Him, for I shall yet praise Him,
>
> The help of my countenance and my God. *(Psalm 42:11, AMP)*

Or in another translation:

> ... For I will again give him thanks, my saving presence and my God. *(Psalm 42:11, NHEB)*

So, here's what I see and hear as I read this psalm.

The psalmist, who has been weeping so much that his tears have been his "food day and night," knows the value of honestly expressing his emotions in God's presence. He doesn't deny the hurt or desperation.

He also knows that the process doesn't end there.

Deep down, the psalmist knows that genuine hope is found in God. He calls on the God he knows from Scripture, and from testimonies passed down. From that anchor, he chooses to trust God with the process as he prays.

He longs to connect with God in prayer. He seems to know that encountering God will transform his understanding and outlook.

He seems to know that, while his feelings are incredibly real, and they are finding valid expression here in the safety of God's presence ... at the same time, they can't be the ultimate source of truth, or provide a solid place to land or build our faith upon.

Here we find the fullness of faithfully wrestling.

For faith to withstand the storms of this world, it has to be built on who God says He is. On His Word. On the Rock of Christ.

The Scripture even says, "For we live by faith, not by sight." (2 Corinthians 5:7, NIV). This saying indicates that sometimes, living in Christ means: reaching *past* interpretations drawn from natural senses & feelings (i.e. "by sight"), which are temporal; to find an eternal, spiritual truth to place our faith in.

We live by faith, which comes by hearing, and hearing by the Word of God. So we ask God: *What do You say is true?*

Follow Psalm 22 in this context. I may have *felt* that God "left me all alone" (Psalm 22:1, CEB) ... But *in reality*, "he didn't hide his face from me. No, he listened when I cried out to him for help." (Psalm 22:24, CEB).

God has never left me or forsaken me. And I have found, as I turn back to God in humility and thanksgiving, remembering His Word ... even if it feels like I can only just barely reach out my hand ... God is always there, and always faithful, and He always meets me there with the grace I need.

With His grace, God upholds me, restores me, and returns to me the joy of my salvation. Time and time again, God shows Himself to be "my saving presence," "the help of my countenance and my God." (Psalm 42:11).

As I have let God into the dark spaces, He has come in and filled them with His healing light. In this, I have found God to be dependable, reliable, and trustworthy. I have found Him to be miraculous.

He clothed Himself with me ... *and then He clothed me with Himself.*

This is so beautiful ... too beautiful to describe ...

Thank God for this gift too wonderful for words! *(2 Corinthians 9:15, NLT)*

Oh, the glorious grace of God.

It may take some time. But friend, it is such a worthwhile process.

So, in conclusion, as we faithfully wrestle through Scripture, let's leave space to breathe deeply, and engage with the light of Christ again... *and again.* This could sound something like:

"Nevertheless, I choose to believe what You say is true. The sun is still shining, even though I don't see it right now in my night. All my life You have been faithful. This is who You say You are, so I choose to accept it as truth. You are always good, and full of abundant grace. And what if Your grace is overflowing to me right now, at this very moment? You say it is. So I will reach out for You in faith that it really is, and receive the grace I need. Thank You, God."

Whatever this looks like to you, here's my encouragement: whatever trust you have to give, place it *in Him*. Rely upon His grace. Believe in His Word.

Because, let us remember, when we welcome the word of grace as the true *Word of God*, it has inherent supernatural power that works effectually within us (1 Thessalonians 2:13). It may not be visible to us right away, but it truly has the power to save our souls:

> ... humbly accept the word God has planted in your hearts, for it has the power to save your souls. *(James 1:21, NLT)*

There is so much hope. And I say this as a man *who used to feel like I had no hope.*

I still struggle, but I bring it before Him. I could tell you so many other stories about that. I hope the few moments I have shared can help you in your journey.

I invite you to make this journey your own and be authentic. I truly believe God can handle it, and wants us to bring it all to Him. Allow yourself to *feel it all* in His loving presence, and let Him into that very space. Let Him fill it with unconditional love. Let the Living Word "become flesh" *in your world.*

And as the Word of Life fills this space, trust Him to transform it.

Allow His countenance to lift yours. Find rest in His smile. Guide your heart back home. Build your house on the Rock. And Let the Word of Christ cause faith to rise. Let it breathe life into you, shape and mold you, even in the hardest places.

Especially in those places.

I believe that great faith is forged by receiving grace: not in the absence of troubles or hard circumstances, but in the presence of them.

I have found precious, priceless eternal treasures in the midst of my most difficult trials.

And I have found that whatever spaces Jesus inhabits, He transforms. He enters in, becomes it fully, and then fully fills it with the glory of Heaven.

> And the Word became flesh and dwelt among us, and we beheld His glory ...
> *(John 1:14, NKJV)*

Oh Father, just as the Word became flesh, may it be unto us now, dwelling in every area of our lives ... and filling us with Your glory.

And oh, the glory ... the sweet surrender of trusting Him, which fills us with life and rest, and joy and peace ...

Consider these beautiful words from the beloved hymn, *'Tis So Sweet to Trust in Jesus*, written by Louisa M. R. Stead (1850-1917):

> 'Tis so sweet to trust in Jesus ... just to take Him at His Word;
>
> Just to rest upon His promise ... just to know, "Thus says the Lord!"[1]

As we hear God speak on this journey, may we truly receive His words for ourselves, *taking Him at His Word*, and experience the sweetness of simply trusting in Him. I pray the roots go down deep into our entire beings.

And when we do receive His words, may we hold onto them tightly.

One last piece of wisdom from dear brother Dwayne:

> If faith is receiving, then great faith is receiving and never letting go.[2]

May we cherish the precious diamond of the word of God's grace, friend, and never let it go.

> Jesus, Jesus, precious Jesus!
>
> O for grace to trust Him more![3]

9

THE INVITATION: AN ENCOUNTER WITH THE GOD OF GRACE

Well, friend, we are finally about to embark.

Ultimately, I do hope that you make this whole journey your own. My phrasing isn't what makes a prayer beautiful. The real diamond is the Scripture behind it. The real diamond is the truth of Christ. And maybe you see fire, brilliance, and sparkle that I don't see!

May the Holy Spirit guide you into all truth, and open your eyes to behold the amazing grace of God.

My greatest joy would be that this book would lead you into your own practice of praying the Scripture, or enrich what you already have, following God for yourself. Explore new Bible translations. Memorize the verses. Become rooted and grounded in grace, truth and love, which are found in Jesus Christ.

Let His words abide in you ... *and cling to the word of grace.*

You never know when it will arise in your heart like a light for your path.

You never know when it will appear in front of you, like water and bread in the desert.

You never know when it will be like a ready sword, equipping you for an unexpected battle.

And, You never know when it may suddenly fill you with wonder ... opening your eyes to the magnificent new creation in Christ ... awakening the faith by which you may enter into God's glorious rest.

Truly, there are so many wonderful reasons to pray the word of grace. Among them is the reality that in it, we finally find the rest for which we were made. In the words of Martin Luther:

> We find no rest for our weary bones unless we cling to the word of grace.[1]

Above all, within these pages, and in praying the word of grace: I pray that you *encounter the God of grace, the Living Word of God.* In Him, we truly find rest for our souls.

At last, let's bring to remembrance once more the words of the famous hymn:

> Amazing grace, how sweet the sound!

As we adventure through these pages together, may we fully experience the bliss and the glory of God's amazing grace, and come to see how sweet the sound truly is.

> How precious is your gracious love, God!
>
> The children of men take refuge in the shadow of your wings.
>
> They are refreshed from the abundance of your house;
>
> You cause them to drink from the river of your pleasures.
>
> *(Psalm 36:7-8, ISV)*

I pray that, in reading through this, you enjoy God, and enjoy grace. Freely, thoroughly, and surprisingly so!

Drink freely from the river of His delights. Take up the light, easy yoke of Jesus. Learn from His gentle, humble heart, and find rest for your soul.

Take refuge in the shadow of His gracious love. Come to His table of grace, which is already set with an open seat for you, and feast on His abundance. Be refreshed. Be filled. Be free.

After all ... if all of this really is true, *then why wouldn't we enjoy it to the fullest?*

This is even what Jesus said He wanted: for us to fully receive His message and His grace, so that we would be *filled to the full with His joy.* (John 15:11, John 16:24, John 17:13, Jeremiah 15:16, Acts 13:52, Romans 15:13, Psalm 16:11, Psalm 21:6, Psalm 68:3)

I would even submit that true gratitude and true humility before God are found in fully receiving and enjoying the gifts He has so generously given to us in Christ.

However one defines grace, this much is clear. Grace comes as a free gift from God. And what do you do with a gift?

You open it. You enjoy it. This is our gratitude. This is the best thing to do with grace!

So. Let's enjoy the overflowing grace of the Lord Jesus Christ together. Let's linger long at the Cross. Let's turn the diamond of God's manifold grace, and watch it sparkle in the light. Let's listen intently for the riveting theme of grace in the symphony of Scripture. Let's partake of the very life of Christ, and enjoy the feast prepared before us.

Let's open our hearts to God, and respond to His compelling invitation:

> Look! I stand at the door and knock. If you hear my voice and open the door, I will come in, and we will share a meal together as friends. *(Revelation 3:20, NLT)*

Are you ready?

PART II

ENJOYING THE FEAST

Psalm 23:5

"You prepare a feast for me ..." (NLT)

Psalm 36:8

"They feast upon the abundance of Your house ..." (NIV)
"They are abundantly satisfied with the fullness of Your house ..." (NKJV)

John 1:16

"For from his fullness we have all received, grace upon grace." (ESV)
"From his abundance we have all received one gracious blessing after another."
(NLT)

〜

Over 200 scriptures, filled with the riches of God's grace.
31 in-depth prayers, crafted from their glory.
Praying the Word of Grace.

1

JESUS: THE WAY TO THE FATHER, THE FULLNESS OF GRACE

*John 1:14, John 1:16, John 1:18,
John 10:30, John 14:20, John 17:26, John 17:21-22,
Ephesians 2:18, Ephesians 3:12, Romans 8:15-16*

John 1:14

And the Word became flesh and dwelt among us, and we have seen his glory, glory as of the only Son from the Father, full of grace and truth. *(ESV)*

The Word became a human [flesh] and lived [made his home; pitched his tabernacle; God's glorious presence dwelt in Israel's tabernacle in the wilderness] among us. We saw his glory [majesty]—the glory that belongs to the only Son [one and only; only begotten] of [who came from] the Father—and he was full of grace and truth [God's gracious love and faithfulness ...] *(EXB)*

John 1:16

For from his fullness we have all received, grace upon grace. *(ESV)*

For out of His fullness [the superabundance of His grace and truth] we have all received grace upon grace [spiritual blessing upon spiritual blessing, favor upon favor, and gift heaped upon gift]. *(AMP)*

From his abundance we have all received one gracious blessing after another. *(NLT)*

John 1:18

No one has ever seen God. The one and only Son, who is himself God and is at the Father's side—he has revealed him. *(CSB)* ... The only begotten Son, who is in the bosom of the Father, He has declared Him. *(NKJV)*

No one has seen God [His essence, His divine nature] at any time; the [One and] only begotten God [that is, the unique Son] who is in the intimate presence of the Father, He has explained Him [and interpreted and revealed the awesome wonder of the Father]. *(AMP)*

John 10:30

I and My Father are one. *(NKJV)*

The Father and I are one. *(NLT)*

John 14:20

On that day you will know that I am in My Father, and you are in Me, and I in you. *(NASB)*

John 17:26

I have made you known to them, and will continue to make you known in order that the love you have for me may be in them and that I myself may be in them. *(NIV)*

I have revealed you to them, and I will continue to do so. Then your love for me will be in them, and I will be in them. *(NLT)*

I have made Your Name known to them and revealed Your character and Your very Self, and I will continue to make [You] known, that the love which You have bestowed upon Me may be in them [felt in their hearts] ... *(AMPC)* ... [overwhelming their heart], and I [may be] in them. *(AMP)* ... and I will live [be] in them. *(EXB)*

John 17:21-22

May they all be one, as you, Father, are in me and I am in you. May they also be in us, so that the world may believe you sent me. I have given them the glory you have given me, so that they may be one as we are one. *(CSB)*

Ephesians 2:18

Now all of us can come to the Father through the same Holy Spirit because of what Christ has done for us. *(NLT)*

We ... have access to the Father through Christ by the one Spirit. *(CEB)*

Ephesians 3:12

Because of Christ and our faith in him, we can now come boldly and confidently into God's presence. *(NLT)*

In Whom, because of our faith in Him, we dare to have the boldness (courage and confidence) of free access (an unreserved approach to God with freedom and without fear). *(AMPC)*

... We can do this through faith in Christ [or because of Christ's faithfulness]. *(EXB)*

Romans 8:15-16

For you have not received a spirit of slavery leading to fear again, but you have received a spirit of adoption as sons and daughters by which we cry out, "Abba! Father!" The Spirit Himself testifies with our spirit that we are children of God. *(NASB)*

... but you have received the Spirit of adoption [the Spirit producing sonship] in [the bliss of] which we cry, Abba (Father)! Father! The Spirit Himself [thus] testifies together with our own spirit, [assuring us] that we are children of God. *(AMPC)*

Praying the Word of Grace

Heavenly Father, I thank You with every fiber of my being! You have fully revealed Yourself through Your only begotten Son, Jesus. He is the Messiah; the Anointed, the Chosen One. He is "God with us." He is the radiance of Your glory, the exact expression of Your being.

I gaze with rapt attention at Jesus, and my heart fills with wonder. In the eyes of Christ, I see the fullness of my Father's indescribable glory. In Him, we see You, for He is one with You. Your divine nature, Your very essence, has been interpreted, explained and shown on full display at last. He is full of grace and truth, and so we know that You are, too. I am captivated by You, awesome, holy, and gracious Father.

Through Jesus, and His glorious revelation, I am filled with Your love. I have been filled with the very same love You have for Jesus, and even filled with all of You, God. Just as You are one with Jesus, so I am one with the Father, Son, and Holy Spirit. God is in me, and I am in God. How wonderful!

I thank You, Father, that through Christ and His faithfulness, I have full and free access to You. I enter into Your presence by the Holy Spirit, with open arms, and with boldness, courage, and confidence. Your love and grace toward me are boundless and unreserved, so I come unreserved to You! I ask that You reveal to me in my innermost being, Father, the truth of my access to You and Your grace. Cause me to know this, so that a childlike boldness and faith may increase within me, and that I would not hold anything back.

I thank You, Father, that I get to enjoy the same intimacy that Jesus Himself has with You. Wow! The Holy Spirit, the spirit of adoption, bears witness to this truth with my own spirit. We sing of Your Father's heart together in harmony. In the bliss of being Your beloved child, I cry out to You, "Abba! Father!"

Jesus said that He has given me the same glory You have given to Him. And from His fullness and abundance, we have all received grace upon grace. I open my arms wide, and step into Your gift, standing under the waterfall of the endless waves of grace. I joyfully accept Your abundance with gratitude! Blessing upon blessing, favor upon favor, and gift heaped upon gift!

Thank You, Gracious Father. I ask that You reveal the truth to me through my entire being, by the limitless power of the Holy Spirit. Cause me to encounter Your love and grace in new ways today, that I may truly know You. May I always be growing in grace and in the knowledge of Jesus, my Lord and Savior. In His name I pray, Amen.

2

FILLED WITH ALL THE FULLNESS OF GOD

John 1:16, Colossians 2:9-10, Ephesians 3:19, Psalm 36:7-8

John 1:16

Indeed, we have all received grace upon grace from his fullness. *(CSB)*

Colossians 2:9-10

For in Him dwells all the fullness of the Godhead bodily; and you are complete in Him, who is the head of all principality and power. *(NKJV)* ... [of every angelic and earthly power]. *(AMP)*

For in Christ lives all the fullness of God in a human body. So you also are complete through your union with Christ, who is the head over every ruler and authority. *(NLT)*

For in him all the wealth of God's being has a living form ... *(BBE)* For the entire fullness of God's nature dwells bodily in Christ, and you have been filled by Him ... *(CSB)*

For in Him all the fullness of Deity (the Godhead) dwells in bodily form [completely expressing the divine essence of God]. And in Him you have been made complete [achieving spiritual stature through Christ] ... *(AMP)*

And you are in Him, made full and having come to fullness of life [in Christ you too are filled with the Godhead—Father, Son and Holy Spirit—and reach full spiritual stature] ... *(AMPC)* and in Christ you have been brought to fullness ... *(NIV)* ... and you have a full and true life in Christ ... *(EXB)*

Ephesians 3:19

I ask that you'll know the love of Christ that is beyond knowledge so that you will be filled entirely with the fullness of God. *(CEB)*

May you experience the love of Christ, though it is too great to understand fully. Then you will be made complete with all the fullness of life and power that comes from God. *(NLT)*

[That you may really come] to know [practically, through experience for yourselves] the love of Christ, which far surpasses mere knowledge [without experience]; that you may be filled [through all your being] unto all the fullness of God [may have the richest measure of the divine Presence, and become a body wholly filled and flooded with God Himself]! *(AMPC)*

... so that you may be made complete as God himself is complete. *(BBE)*

Psalm 36:7-8

How precious is Your lovingkindness, O God!
Therefore the children of men put their trust under the shadow of Your wings.
They are abundantly satisfied with the fullness of Your house,
And You give them drink from the river of Your pleasures. *(NKJV)*

They are filled from the abundance of Your house;
You let them drink from Your refreshing stream. *(HCSB)*
... from the river of Your delights. *(NASB)*
... from your river of pure joy. *(CEB)*

Praying the Word of Grace

Heavenly Father, I thank You for Your abundant gift, that I have indeed received grace upon grace from the very fullness of Jesus Christ!

Jesus, You are King! You are the head over all principality and power, every ruler and authority, in the heavens and on the earth. In You, all the fullness of the Godhead dwells in a human body. In Christ, the total divine nature and essence of God – all the wealth of God's being – has a living form.

And Jesus, through Your finished work and receiving the abundance of Your grace, I have been completely united with You for eternity! Through my union with You, I have been made complete, as God Himself is complete. In Christ, I have been brought to the fullness of life. I share in Your full spiritual stature and capacity, as I am one with You. Oh, the paradise, the bliss of being one with You!

Father, I thank You that in Christ, I too am filled with the Godhead—Father, Son and Holy Spirit. What a marvelous, life-altering reality! I ask that You open the eyes of my heart to this reality, Father, so that I may wholeheartedly live this "full and true life," which is mine through Christ Jesus.

Father, I long for fresh encounters with You. I ask that You make me more aware of Your presence, so that moment by moment, I can experience the matchless love of Christ. I ask that I encounter the Holy Spirit as I read Your Scripture, and in everyday moments.

I ask this so that more and more, I may truly come to know Your love, through experiencing it for myself, surpassing all previous knowledge I have. And through this, I am being filled entirely, through all my being, with all the fullness of God.

Through Christ, I am made complete with all the fullness of life and power that comes from God. I have the richest measure of Your divine presence. I have a body wholly filled and flooded with God Himself.

How precious is Your loving-kindness, O God! I am abundantly satisfied with the fullness of Your house. I put my trust under the shadow of Your wings. Thank You for always giving me refreshing drink from the river of Your pleasures, the stream of Your delights. I am filled to the full with pure joy and ecstasy! In union with Christ, I pray, and in His wonderful name. Amen.

3

ENTRUSTED TO GOD AND TO THE WORD OF HIS GRACE

Acts 20:32, Colossians 1:5-6, Romans 1:16, Luke 2:14, John 15:3, John 17:17, Ephesians 5:25-26, Acts 20:24

Acts 20:32

Now I entrust you to God and the message of his grace, which is able to build you up and give you an inheritance among all whom God has made holy. *(CEB)*

And now I commend you to God [placing you in His protective, loving care] and [I commend you] to the word of His grace [the counsel and promises of His unmerited favor]. His grace is able to build you up and to give you the [rightful] inheritance among all those who are sanctified [that is, among those who are set apart for God's purpose—all believers]. *(AMP)*

Colossians 1:5-6

You have this faith and love because of the hope reserved for you in heaven. You previously heard about this hope through the true message, the good news, which has come to you. This message has been bearing fruit and growing among you since the day you heard and truly understood God's grace, in the same way that it is bearing fruit and growing in the whole world. *(CEB)*

... You have had this expectation ever since you first heard the truth of the Good News. This same Good News that came to you is going out all over the world. It is bearing fruit everywhere by changing lives, just as it changed your lives from the day you first heard and understood the truth about God's wonderful grace. *(NLT)*

... Everywhere in the world that Good News [Gospel] is bringing blessings [bearing fruit] and is growing ... *(EXB)*

Romans 1:16

For I am not ashamed of the gospel of Christ, for it is the power of God to salvation for everyone who believes ... *(NKJV)*

Luke 2:14

Suddenly, there was with the angel a multitude of the heavenly host praising God, and saying, "Glory to God in the highest, and on earth peace, good will toward humankind." *(NHEB)*

John 15:3

Now ye are clean through the word which I have spoken unto you. *(KJV)*

You have already been pruned and purified by the message I have given you. *(NLT)*

John 17:17

Sanctify them in the truth; Your word is truth. *(NASB)*

Make them holy by the true word: your word is the true word. *(BBE)*

Sanctify them [purify, consecrate, separate them for Yourself, make them holy] by the Truth; Your Word is Truth. *(AMPC)*

Ephesians 5:25-26

For husbands, this means love your wives, just as Christ loved the church. He gave up his life for her to make her holy and clean, washed by the cleansing of God's word. *(NLT)*

... Christ loved the church and gave himself up for her to make her holy, cleansing her by the washing with water through the word. *(NIV)*

Acts 20:24

But my life is worth nothing to me unless I use it for finishing the work assigned me by the Lord Jesus—the work of telling others the Good News about the wonderful grace of God. *(NLT)*

... so that I may finish my race with joy, and the ministry which I received from the Lord Jesus, to fully testify to the Good News of the grace of God. *(WEB)*

Praying the Word of Grace

Oh, Wonderful Heavenly Father, how richly You have blessed me! I have been given this remarkable privilege of hearing and knowing Your word of grace. Your servants and apostles have given their lives over centuries to tell the world of Your glorious Good News. Because of Your favor and power at work through them, I now stand firm in this grace. I am amazed and my heart spills over with gratitude!

I have been entrusted to Your loving, protective care, Father. I rest in Your tender, strong embrace. I have also been committed to the word of grace, the glorious gospel of Jesus Christ. This message of grace is true, and is able to build me up and strengthen me. The word of Your grace is able to give me the inheritance which is rightfully mine through Christ, among all the saints, who are the people set apart for Your purposes.

I thank You, Father, for this word of Your wonderful grace, which fills me with faith, hope and love. This message is always growing and bearing fruit. As it spreads throughout the world, it is always bringing blessings and changing lives. It has changed my life forever, from the day I first heard. I pray that, through the revelation of Your Holy Spirit, I would fully understand the truth about Your grace: Your heart and good intent, all You have accomplished, and all I have been given by the grace of God.

I am so honored to carry this gospel within me. It is the most beautiful sound to my ears, and it resonates deep within my being. With all Your heavenly angels, I sing the echo of their chorus in my heart: "Glory to God in the highest, and on earth peace, good will toward humankind." Embolden me and empower me, and open doors for me to tell others about the wonderful grace of God.

Father, how precious is Your Word. Through the words that Jesus has spoken, I have been made clean. Oh, how glorious! I already have been cleansed and washed, purified and made holy. Through Your word, I have also been pruned and trimmed like a tree, so that I may bear spiritual fruit in greater abundance. You have sanctified me, consecrated me, set me part for Yourself, in Your truth. Your word is truth. I stand on Your Word, and so I stand on holy ground.

Father, I ask for You to fill me with intimate knowledge of Your grace and truth, by the Holy Spirit. He is the Spirit of grace and truth, who lives within me. Open my heart to experience the riches of the glorious Good News of Jesus Christ, in all its greatness. In Christ's name I pray, amen.

4

THE INHERITANCE OF THE SAINTS IN LIGHT

*Acts 20:32, Ephesians 1:11, Titus 3:7, John 17:3, Psalm 16:5-6,
Ephesians 1:14, Ephesians 1:17-19, Colossians 1:11-12*

Acts 20:32

And now I commend you to God, and to the word of his grace, which is able to build you up, and to give you the inheritance among all them that are sanctified. *(ASV)*

And now, I give you into the care of God and the word of his grace, which is able to make you strong and to give you your heritage among all the saints. *(BBE)*

Ephesians 1:11

Furthermore, because we are united with Christ, we have received an inheritance from God, for he chose us in advance, and he makes everything work out according to his plan. *(NLT)*

We have also received an inheritance in Christ... *(CEB)*

Titus 3:7

So, since we have been made righteous by his grace, we can inherit the hope for eternal life. *(CEB)*

So that, having been given righteousness through grace, we might have a part in the heritage, the hope of eternal life. *(BBE)*

John 17:3

And this is eternal life, that they may know You, the only true God, and Jesus Christ whom You have sent. *(NKJV)*

Psalm 16:5-6

LORD, You are my portion
and my cup of blessing;
You hold my future.
The boundary lines have fallen for me
in pleasant places;
indeed, I have a beautiful inheritance. *(HCSB)*

O Lord, You are the portion of my inheritance and my cup;
You maintain my lot ... *(NKJV)*

Ephesians 1:14

The Holy Spirit is the down payment of our inheritance, until the redemption of the possession, to the praise of his glory. *(CSB)*

That [Spirit] is the guarantee of our inheritance [the firstfruits, the pledge and foretaste, the down payment on our heritage], in anticipation of its full redemption and our acquiring [complete] possession of it—to the praise of His glory. *(AMPC)*

Ephesians 1:17-19

I pray that the God of our Lord Jesus Christ, the glorious Father, would give you the Spirit of wisdom and revelation in the knowledge of him. I pray that the eyes of your heart may be enlightened so that you may know what is the hope of his calling, what is the wealth of his glorious inheritance in the saints, and what is the immeasurable greatness of his power toward us who believe, according to the mighty working of his strength. *(CSB)*

[For I always pray to] the God of our Lord Jesus Christ, the Father of glory, that He may grant you a spirit of wisdom and revelation [of insight into mysteries and secrets] in the [deep and intimate] knowledge of Him... *(AMPC)*

... And [I pray] that the eyes of your heart [the very center and core of your being] may be enlightened [flooded with light by the Holy Spirit], so that you will know and cherish the hope [the divine guarantee, the confident expectation] to which He has called you, the riches of His glorious inheritance in the saints (God's people), and [so that you will begin to know] what the immeasurable and unlimited and surpassing greatness of His [active, spiritual] power is in us who believe... *(AMP)*

Colossians 1:11-12

May you be strengthened with all power, according to His glorious might, for all endurance and patience, with joy giving thanks to the Father, who has enabled you to share in the saints' inheritance in the light. *(HCSB)*

God will strengthen you [...being strengthened] with his own great power [all power according to his glorious might] so that you will not give up when troubles come, but you will be patient. And you will joyfully give thanks [or ...have patience with joy, giving thanks] to the Father who has made you able to have a share in all that he has prepared for his people in the kingdom of light [the inheritance of the saints/holy ones in the light]. *(EXB)*

... He made it so you could take part in the inheritance ... *(CEB)*

PRAYING THE WORD OF GRACE

Heavenly Father, I am so delighted and grateful. My cup overflows! I have been given into Your tender, loving care, and I am given to the word of grace. In it, I am built up and made strong. Through it, I receive my portion of the inheritance of the saints in the light.

I thank You that, through my union with Christ, I have received an inheritance from You, Father, along with every other person who trusts in the name of Jesus. You enabled me to take part in this bountiful, glorious inheritance through Christ, and in doing so, You accomplished exactly what You had always had in mind. You had chosen me in advance for this bounty of grace and goodwill.

Since I have been made righteous by Your grace, I have become a co-heir with Christ, and I inherit a beautiful, imperishable blessing from Heaven's infinite supply. The blessings of eternal life, and hope therein, are mine forever.

And the greatest gift is knowing You, Father. This is eternal life. You are the true portion of my inheritance. You are my cup of blessing which runs over. You are the only true God and Creator of the Heavens and the Earth, and I get to intimately know You as my "Abba" Father. Oh how indescribable is Your love! How immeasurably beautiful it is to really know You, and Your Son whom You sent, and the Holy Spirit whom You gave. You are mine, and I am Yours! How extravagantly You have loved me and blessed me!

And I have yet to unveil so much of this glorious inheritance in the saints. I rejoice that it is mine forever! I thank You that my allotment is secure in You, and that You hold my future. I thank You that the boundary lines of my promised land are all in pleasant places. Your plans for me are good, and filled with hope. Father, lead me into the joy of my promise. Give me eyes to see, that I may explore this glorious territory that You have given me in Christ, adventuring and delighting in it with You, and Jesus, and Holy Spirit!

Thank You Father, for the gift of the Holy Spirit, whom You gave to me, poured out through Christ, who finished the work and sat down at Your right hand. Holy Spirit, You are the guarantee, the first fruits of this inheritance. You give me divine confidence and hope. You cause me to joyfully anticipate the fullness and complete redemption of Christ's reward. And Father, You are glorified most when I fully receive Your gift! So I open my arms, and respond from my spirit with an ecstatic, "Yes! Thank You! And amen!"

I earnestly pray that the eyes of my heart would be flooded with light by the Holy Spirit. In Your light, may I see light in the core of my being, so that I would know and cherish the hope I have; the riches of Your glorious inheritance; and know what is the immeasurable, unlimited greatness of Your power which is working in me, according to Your strength.

With this great hope in mind, I can endure all things with patience, joy, and gratitude. Knowing all I have, and Who is in me – the Giver and His immeasurable gift – fills me with grace for all things. I ask for the spirit of wisdom and revelation, to intimately know You, Your power, Your love, and the infinite hope that is in Christ. In His name I pray, Amen.

5

THE GRACE IS WITH US

2 Timothy 4:22, 2 John 1:3, 2 Peter 1:2,
John 14:27, Romans 16:20, 2 Corinthians 13:14

2 Timothy 4:22

The Lord Jesus Christ is with thy spirit; the grace is with you!
Amen. *(YLT)*

The Lord Jesus Christ be with your spirit. Grace (God's favor and blessing) be
with you. Amen (so be it). *(AMPC)*

2 John 1:3

Grace, mercy, and peace will be with us, from God the Father, and from the
Lord Jesus Christ, the Son of the Father, in truth and love. *(WEB)* ... in all true
love. *(BBE)*

Grace, mercy, and peace (inner calm, a sense of spiritual well-being) will be
with us, from God the Father and from Jesus Christ, the Father's Son, in truth
and love. *(AMP)*

2 Peter 1:2

Grace and peace be multiplied unto you through the knowledge of God, and of Jesus our Lord *(KJV)*

Grace and peace be yours in abundance ... *(NIV)* Grace to you and peace be accomplished ... *(DRA)* May grace and peace ever be increasing in you ... *(BBE)*

John 14:27

I am leaving you with a gift—peace of mind and heart. And the peace I give is a gift the world cannot give. So don't be troubled or afraid. *(NLT)*

Peace I leave with you; My [perfect] peace I give to you; not as the world gives do I give to you. Do not let your heart be troubled, nor let it be afraid. [Let My perfect peace calm you in every circumstance and give you courage and strength for every challenge.] *(AMP)*

Romans 16:20

And the God of peace will quickly crush Satan under your feet. The grace of our Lord Jesus Christ be with you. *(WEB)*

The God who brings [of] peace will soon defeat Satan and give you power over him [crush Satan under your feet] ... *(EXB)*

... The [wonderful] grace of our Lord Jesus be with you. *(AMP)*

2 Corinthians 13:14

The grace of the Lord Jesus Christ, and the love of God, and the communion of the Holy Spirit, be with you all. *(ASV)* ... and the harmony of the Holy Spirit, be with you all. *(BBE)*

The grace (favor and spiritual blessing) of the Lord Jesus Christ and the love of God and the presence and fellowship (the communion and sharing together, and participation) in the Holy Spirit be with you all. Amen (so be it). *(AMPC)*

Praying the Word of Grace

Magnificent Heavenly Father, I give You all my praise and worship! I thank You from the depths of my heart, for You have blessed us beyond anything we could ever think or imagine! I take time to open Your gifts:

The Lord Jesus Christ is with my spirit. God's amazing grace is with me. Grace, mercy and peace are with me abundantly, from God the Father, and from the Lord Jesus Christ, the Father's Son, in all true love. I take time in Your presence to allow that to sink in.

In Christ, You have given me true peace: Your perfect peace, an inner calm and spiritual well-being, in truth and love. Your peace is beyond anything in this world, and it is ever-increasing to me, along with Your grace.

And the God of peace – the One who brings peace – will quickly crush Satan under my feet! You have defeated the enemy, and give me power over him. You trample him in every area of my life. So I will not let my heart be afraid or troubled, because Your peace calms me and gives me courage.

I am surrounded by the wonderful grace, divine favor, and spiritual blessing of the Lord Jesus Christ; and the unconditional love of God the Father; and the presence and fellowship, the communion and sharing together, and the participation in the Holy Spirit; together with all believers. We have been placed in Christ, miraculously united in Him as one. May the beautiful harmony of the Holy Spirit be with us all!

Father, I ask that You open the eyes of my heart, with all Your children, so we can see all that we truly have. Cause my heart to become so aware of the presence and communion of the Holy Spirit that I share in.

I surrender to the blissful dance of Father, Son and Holy Spirit, that I have been invited into by grace. I open my hands with childlike trust to receive the grace that is already with me: Your unconditional blessings, favor and power. I receive Christ Himself, who is in me and with my spirit.

I give all my cares to You, Father, allowing Your perfect peace and inner calm, which surpasses all understanding, to guard my heart and mind in Christ Jesus. Oh how sweet it is to trust in You, that Your word is true. Your love really knows no limits. Your mercies never come to an end. Your grace overflows through the hands of Jesus. In His name I pray, Amen.

6

GROWING IN GRACE

2 Peter 3:18, 2 Peter 1:2, 1 Peter 2:2-3, 2 Timothy 2:1

2 Peter 3:18

But grow in the grace and knowledge of our Lord and Savior Jesus Christ. To him be the glory both now and forever. Amen. *(WEB)*

But grow [spiritually mature] in the grace and knowledge of our Lord and Savior Jesus Christ. To Him be glory (honor, majesty, splendor), both now and to the day of eternity. Amen. *(AMP)*

But be increased in grace and in the knowledge of our Lord and Saviour Jesus Christ. May he have glory now and for ever. So be it. *(BBE)*

2 Peter 1:2

Grace and peace be multiplied unto you through the knowledge of God, and of Jesus our Lord *(KJV)*

Grace and peace be yours in abundance ... *(NIV)* Grace to you and peace be accomplished ... *(DRA)* May grace and peace ever be increasing in you ... *(BBE)*

[May] Grace and peace be given to you more and more [lavished upon you; multiplied to you], because you truly know [or as you grow in your knowledge; through/in the knowledge of] God and Jesus our Lord. *(EXB)*

May grace (God's favor) and peace (which is perfect well-being, all necessary good, all spiritual prosperity, and freedom from fears and agitating passions and moral conflicts) be multiplied to you in [the full, personal, precise, and correct] knowledge of God and of Jesus our Lord. *(AMPC)*

1 Peter 2:2-3

As newborn babies, long for the pure milk of the Word, that with it you may grow, if indeed you have tasted that the Lord is gracious *(WEB)*

As newborn babies want milk, you should want the pure [sincere; unadulterated] and simple [or spiritual] teaching [milk]. By it you can mature [grow; reach maturity] in your salvation, because you have already examined and seen [tasted] how good the Lord is ... *(EXB)* ... Since you have [already] tasted the goodness and kindness of the Lord. *(AMPC)*

2 Timothy 2:1

So, my child, draw your strength from the grace that is in Christ Jesus. *(CEB)*

So you, my son, be strong [constantly strengthened] and empowered in the grace that is [to be found only] in Christ Jesus. *(AMP)*

Praying the Word of Grace

Heavenly Father, I thank You for Your boundless gift of grace, given to me through Your Son, Jesus Christ. I position myself to receive more and more from Your infinite supply.

I thank You that grace and peace are multiplied unto me. They are given to me more and more, and they are ever increasing in me, for You lavish them upon me in abundance.

Father, I ask that I would grow in the true, intimate knowledge of You, and of Jesus, and of the Holy Spirit. I trust You to reveal Yourself to me in a way that is full, personal, precise, and correct. As I come to know You more, I spiritually mature and grow in the grace in which I now stand, like a tree whose roots go down deeper into rich soil.

I thank You that Your grace constantly empowers me. I draw my strength from Your grace, found only in Jesus.

I thank You that Your peace is also ever-increasing in me. In Your peace, I have perfect well-being, all necessary good, all spiritual prosperity, and freedom from fears, and agitating passions and moral conflicts. Your peace is perfect, and it guards my whole life.

I rejoice with all of my being! I have tasted how good and gracious You are. I have examined and I have seen Your radical goodness and kindness. And I am yearning to grow in grace and my knowledge of You.

Therefore, just as newborn babies want pure milk, I long for the pure milk of the Word. I ask for You to increase my desire for the pure, sincere, unadulterated, and simple spiritual teaching of grace. I thank You that, as I partake of this Word of grace, I am powerfully growing and maturing in my salvation. I am strengthened by Your grace.

Father, I ask that You show me areas where I can grow in grace and in my knowledge of You. Whisper revelation to my innermost being throughout my days, and put me in the path of people who speak grace and truth.

All the glory, honor, majesty, and splendor be unto You, both now and to the day of eternity, forever and ever. Praise the holy, powerful, wondrous name of Jesus Christ! Amen!

7

THE RICHES OF GOD'S GRACE

Ephesians 1:5-8, Ephesians 2:6-7

Ephesians 1:5-8

He predestined us to be adopted as sons through Jesus Christ for himself, according to the good pleasure of his will, to the praise of his glorious grace that he lavished on us in the Beloved One.

In him we have redemption through his blood, the forgiveness of our trespasses, according to the riches of his grace that he richly poured out on us with all wisdom and understanding. *(CSB)*

God decided in advance to adopt us into his own family by bringing us to himself through Jesus Christ. This is what he wanted to do, and it gave him great pleasure. So we praise God for the glorious grace he has poured out on us who belong to his dear Son. He is so rich in kindness and grace that he purchased our freedom with the blood of his Son and forgave our sins. He has showered his kindness on us, along with all wisdom and understanding. *(NLT)*

For He foreordained us (destined us, planned in love for us) to be adopted (revealed) as His own children through Jesus Christ, in accordance with the purpose of His will [because it pleased Him and was His kind intent]—[So that we might be] to the praise and the commendation of His glorious grace (favor and mercy), which He so freely bestowed on us in the Beloved ... *(AMPC)*

... In Christ [him] we are set free [have been redeemed/purchased] by the blood of his death [his blood; blood signifies his sacrificial death], and so we have forgiveness of sins. How rich is [or This redemption reveals the wealth of; ... according to the riches of] God's grace, which he has given to us so fully and freely [lavished on us] ... *(EXB)*

Ephesians 2:6-7

Together with Christ Jesus He also raised us up and seated us in the heavens, so that in the coming ages He might display the immeasurable riches of His grace through His kindness to us in Christ Jesus. *(HCSB)*

And hath raised us up together, and hath made us sit together in the heavenly places, through Christ Jesus. That he might shew in the ages to come the abundant riches of his grace, in his bounty towards us in Christ Jesus. *(DRA)*

... He did this that He might clearly demonstrate through the ages to come the immeasurable (limitless, surpassing) riches of His free grace (His unmerited favor) in [His] kindness and goodness of heart toward us in Christ Jesus. *(AMPC)*

... God did this to show future generations the greatness of his grace by the goodness that God has shown us in Christ Jesus. *(CEB)*

Praying the Word of Grace

Generous Father in Heaven, I freely welcome Your rich, wonderful grace, love, and kindness into my heart, knowing that freedom is found in receiving all You have to offer.

When I think of the depths of Your love, I am just astounded. You always had the plan of fully embracing me as Your dearly loved child, and placing me in

Christ, the Beloved One. I have been fully revealed as a child of God, according to the good pleasure of Your will. This is what you always wanted. This was Your kind intent, and it gave You great pleasure. How amazing Your heart is!

Oh how wonderful is Your glorious grace that You lavished upon me! You have showered me with Your kindness in the Beloved One, Your Son. And I am accepted as a part of Your Beloved. I give honor and praise to Your grace, favor and mercy, and I let gratitude pour forth from my heart!

Let my life be a living testimony of Your grace!

You are so rich in grace and kindness, that You purchased my freedom, my eternal redemption, even my very life, with the precious, priceless blood of Your Son. You forgave my sins, and restored me. You have set me free!

This was all according to the riches of Your grace, which You richly poured out on me, with all wisdom and understanding.

The riches of Your grace are immeasurable, limitless and surpassing. Through the riches of Your grace, I have been raised together with Christ, and seated in the Heavens with Him. How amazing! I am seated with Christ in Heavenly places! What a bounty of love, what abundance of grace You have displayed!

Through these irreplaceable gifts toward us, Your children, You have displayed to all future generations the greatness of Your free grace, through Your kindness and goodness of heart toward us in Christ Jesus.

I ask, Wonderful Father, that You release wisdom and understanding within my heart, mind, and spirit, to fully know all the riches of Your grace. May I come to know the depths of Your kindness, and come to see the plan in Your heart, so that I may fully partake in all that You have paid for through the precious blood of Your Son, Jesus. It gave You great joy to give this grace, so I want to receive it with joy, that I may be radiant with Your grace, and display to the world what a kind, good Father You are. In Christ, the Beloved, I pray. Amen.

8

THE GRACE EXCHANGE

2 Corinthians 8:9, 2 Corinthians 5:21, John 3:16,
1 Peter 2:24, Isaiah 53:5, John 19:30

2 Corinthians 8:9

For you know the grace of our Lord Jesus Christ, that though He was rich, yet for your sake He became poor, so that you through His poverty might become rich. *(NASB)*

For you are becoming progressively acquainted with and recognizing more strongly and clearly the grace of our Lord Jesus Christ (His kindness, His gracious generosity, His undeserved favor and spiritual blessing), [in] that though He was [so very] rich, yet for your sakes He became [so very] poor, in order that by His poverty you might become enriched (abundantly supplied). *(AMPC)*

2 Corinthians 5:21

God caused the one who didn't know sin to be sin for our sake so that through him we could become the righteousness of God. *(CEB)*

For our sake He made Christ [virtually] to be sin Who knew no sin, so that in and through Him we might become [endued with, viewed as being in, and examples of] the righteousness of God [what we ought to be, approved and acceptable and in right relationship with Him, by His goodness]. *(AMPC)* [... by His gracious lovingkindness]. *(AMP)*

John 3:16

For God so loved the world that he gave his one and only Son, that whoever believes in him shall not perish but have eternal life. *(NIV)*

For God so greatly loved and dearly prized the world that He [even] gave up His only begotten (unique) Son, so that whoever believes in (trusts in, clings to, relies on) Him shall not perish (come to destruction, be lost) but have eternal (everlasting) life. *(AMPC)*

1 Peter 2:24

He himself bore our sins in his body on the tree; so that, having died to sins, we might live for righteousness. By his wounds you have been healed. *(CSB)*

He took our sins on himself, giving his body to be nailed on the tree, so that we, being dead to sin, might have a new life in righteousness, and by his wounds we have been made well. *(BBE)*

... He Himself brought our sins in His body up on the cross ... *(NASB)* He personally carried our sins in His body on the cross [willingly offering Himself on it, as on an altar of sacrifice], so that we might die to sin [becoming immune from the penalty and power of sin] and live for righteousness ... *(AMP)* ... by whose stripes you were healed. *(NKJV)*

Isaiah 53:5

But he was pierced for our rebellion,
crushed for our sins.
He was beaten so we could be whole.
He was whipped so we could be healed. *(NLT)*

But he was pierced for our transgressions;
he was crushed for our iniquities;
upon him was the chastisement that brought us peace,
and with his wounds we are healed. *(ESV)*

But He was wounded for our transgressions, He was bruised for our guilt and iniquities; the chastisement [needful to obtain] peace and well-being for us was upon Him, and with the stripes [that wounded] Him we are healed and made whole. *(AMPC)*

John 19:30

When he had received the drink, Jesus said, "It is finished." ... *(NIV)* ... "[completed; accomplished]." ... *(EXB)* ... All is done. And with his head bent he gave up his spirit. *(BBE)*

Praying the Word of Grace

Gracious Heavenly Father, through Your revelation by the Holy Spirit, I am becoming more and more acquainted with the grace of our Lord Jesus Christ, Your Son. Thank You for enabling me to recognize, with greater clarity and strength, Your kindness, Your gracious generosity, Your undeserved favor and spiritual blessing, and the power of this grace You have so freely bestowed upon us. I ask that, by that same grace and revelation, I would come to know it even deeper now.

Father, I stand in awe at Your amazing love. You so greatly loved the world – You so dearly prized us – that You even gave up Your only begotten Son for us. You did this for us, so that whoever believes in Him shall not perish, but have everlasting life. This grace takes my breath away.

Jesus, what a sacrifice, too holy, too powerful for words! Oh Holy Spirit, give me revelation, help me to encounter and embrace the power of the Cross of Jesus Christ. Help me to know, by intimately encountering You, the depths of what truly happened there. Jesus, I cling to You as my Savior! I rely on You, and I trust in You. You rescued me from destruction. I am no longer lost. I am found in You.

Jesus, You lived in the abundant riches of Heaven's wealth. Yet, You put it all aside for my sake, and became so very poor, so that through Your poverty I might become rich, and abundantly supplied by Your grace.

You knew no sin at all, yet the Father caused You to actually be sin for my sake, so that in and through You I might become the righteousness of God. In the great exchange at the Cross of Christ, You took my sin, and gave me Your righteousness. I have become endued with righteousness. I am set right, I am approved and accepted by God, and made what I ought to be. All because of You.

You actually brought our sins in Your body up on the Cross, willingly offering Yourself on it, as on an altar of sacrifice. Now, we are dead to sin, and alive with a new life in righteousness.

Jesus, on the Cross, You uttered the words, "it is finished," signifying the entire work of salvation had been completed by You. Sin and all its effects were taken on by You completely, and in You, there is immunity from the penalty and power of sin. By Your stripes – by Your wounds – we have been healed!

Jesus, You were beaten so we could be whole. You were whipped so we could be healed. The crushing and piercing You endured for our sins were fully sufficient for us in bringing us complete peace and well-being!

The healing and wholeness for my entire being – body, soul and spirit – have been purchased completely, accomplished and finished, at the Cross of Christ. By His wounds, I have been made whole! Father, I thank You for this miraculous truth, and I ask that You cause me to know the truth deeper still.

Father, this was all Your doing, from Your goodness and Your gracious lovingkindness. Thank You for the immeasurable gift of Your Son, and eternal life through Him. In His name, I pray. Amen.

9

SAVED BY GRACE ALONE

Ephesians 1:7-8, Romans 3:23-24,
Ephesians 2:8-9, Titus 3:4-8

Ephesians 1:7-8

In Him we have redemption through His blood, the forgiveness of sins, according to the riches of His grace, which He made to abound toward us ... *(NKJV)*

... according to the riches of his grace, which he lavished upon us, in all wisdom and insight. *(ESV)* ... through the wealth of his grace, which he gave us in full measure in all wisdom and care. *(BBE)*

We have been ransomed through his Son's blood, and we have forgiveness for our failures based on his overflowing grace, which he poured over us with wisdom and understanding. *(CEB)*

Romans 3:23-24

For all have sinned, and come short of the glory of God; Being justified freely by his grace through the redemption that is in Christ Jesus. *(KJV)*

... but all are treated as righteous freely by his grace because of a ransom that was paid by Christ Jesus. *(CEB)*

... [All] are justified and made upright and in right standing with God, freely and gratuitously by His grace (His unmerited favor and mercy), through the redemption which is [provided] in Christ Jesus *(AMPC)*

Ephesians 2:8-9

For by grace you have been saved through faith, and that not of yourselves; it is the gift of God, not of works, lest anyone should boast. *(NKJV)*

... you have been saved by grace through believing [faith]. You did not save yourselves; it was a gift from God. It was not the result of your own efforts [works], so you cannot [no one can] brag about it [boast]. *(EXB)*

For it is by grace [God's remarkable compassion and favor drawing you to Christ] that you have been saved [actually delivered from judgment and given eternal life] through faith. And this [salvation] is not of yourselves [not through your own effort], but it is the [undeserved, gracious] gift of God; not as a result of [your] works [nor your attempts to keep the Law], so that no one will [be able to] boast or take credit in any way [for his salvation]. *(AMP)*

Titus 3:4-8

But "when God our savior's kindness and love appeared, he saved us because of his mercy, not because of righteous things we had done. He did it through the washing of new birth and the renewing by the Holy Spirit, which God poured out upon us generously through Jesus Christ our savior. So, since we have been made righteous by his grace, we can inherit the hope for eternal life." This saying is reliable ... *(CEB)*

But when the kindness and love [love of humanity] of God our Savior was shown [appeared; was revealed], he saved us because of his mercy. It was not because of good deeds we did to be right with him [or righteous deeds we did]. He saved us through the washing that made us new people [of new-birth/re-generation and renewal] through [by] the Holy Spirit. God poured out richly [generously; abundantly] upon us that Holy Spirit through Jesus Christ our Savior. Being [...so that having been] made right with God [justified; declared righteous] by his grace, we could have the hope of receiving [become heirs with the hope/expectation of] the life that never ends [eternal life]. This teaching is true [saying/word is trustworthy] ... *(EXB)*

... so that we would be justified [made free of the guilt of sin] by His [compassionate, undeserved] grace, and that we would be [acknowledged as acceptable to Him and] made heirs of eternal life [actually experiencing it] according to our hope (His guarantee). This is a faithful and trustworthy saying. *(AMP)*

Praying the Word of Grace

Oh Righteous and Merciful Heavenly Father; my God, and my Savior! Your kindness and love for humanity have appeared and have been fully revealed through Your Son Jesus!

You saved us, not because of any good things we have done, but because of Your great mercy. You came to our rescue because of the great love with which You loved us.

We all sinned, and we came short of Your glory. However, by Your grace, through the redemption provided in Him and ransom He paid, I have been freely and completely justified. You have gratuitously and generously given me Your grace, favor and mercy. I have right standing with You, and I have been made upright.

In Christ, I have redemption through His blood, and the forgiveness of all my sins and failures. This priceless gift – all that is in Christ – is mine, with no limits! Yes, it comes through the infinite wealth of Your grace, which You lavished on me, poured out over me, and gave me in full measure, in all wisdom, care, and understanding. Your grace is overflowing and it abounds toward me!

Father, I thank You for Your unfathomable gift: I have been saved by grace, through believing in Christ and His finished work. It is by Your remarkable compassion, and Your favor drawing me to Christ, that I was actually delivered from all sin and judgment, and given eternal life. It is an undeserved, gracious gift from You, Father. It was not given as a result of my own merit, nor my works or attempts to keep the Law, so I take no credit. I have been saved by grace alone, through faith.

You saved me through the new birth, and the renewing by the Holy Spirit, which You poured out upon me generously and abundantly through Jesus Christ, our Savior. By the Holy Spirit, I have been washed, made into a new person, regenerated and renewed, and brought to new life. I have been declared righteous, made free from sin and the guilt of sin, and accepted into Your arms, by Your compassionate, undeserved grace. I have been made an heir, inheriting the hope of eternal life, and actually experiencing it by the Spirit of God.

Father, I thank You that this is a faithful and trustworthy saying. This teaching is true.

Oh Father, I surrender to the overwhelming deluge of grace upon grace! And I rejoice! For there is absolutely nothing I can boast about in my salvation. I did nothing to save myself. I cannot even boast in my faith, for all is a gift from Your hands. My very life, the breath in my lungs I have used to speak Your name, and my new life in Christ ... all are from Your hands, Father. Nothing came from me. It is all of You, to Your glory!

Father, I am so happy to be called Your child, and set free, by Your grace. I pray You would open my heart to these truths, and establish me in the joy of salvation in Christ Jesus, and the riches of Your grace. I pray all this in His wonderful name, Amen.

1 0

CONTINUING IN GRACE

Colossians 2:6-7, Acts 11:23, Acts 13:43, Hebrews 13:7-9

Colossians 2:6-7

Therefore, as you have received Christ Jesus the Lord, so walk in Him, having been firmly rooted and now being built up in Him and established in your faith, just as you were instructed, and overflowing with gratitude. *(NASB)*

And now, just as you accepted Christ Jesus as your Lord, you must continue to follow him. Let your roots grow down into him, and let your lives be built on him. Then your faith will grow strong in the truth you were taught, and you will overflow with thankfulness. *(NLT)*

As you have therefore received Christ, [even] Jesus the Lord, [so] walk (regulate your lives and conduct yourselves) in union with and conformity to Him. Have the roots [of your being] firmly and deeply planted [in Him, fixed and founded in Him], being continually built up in Him, becoming increasingly more confirmed and established in the faith, just as you were taught, and abounding and overflowing in it with thanksgiving. *(AMPC)*

Acts 11:23

Then when he arrived and witnessed the grace of God, he rejoiced and began to encourage them all with resolute heart to remain true to the Lord *(NASB)*

When he arrived and saw what grace (favor) God was bestowing upon them, he was full of joy; and he continuously exhorted (warned, urged, and encouraged) them all to cleave unto and remain faithful to and devoted to the Lord with [resolute and steady] purpose of heart. *(AMPC)*

Acts 13:43

Now when the congregation had broken up, many of the Jews and devout proselytes followed Paul and Barnabas, who, speaking to them, persuaded them to continue in the grace of God. *(NKJV)*

... Paul and Barnabas were persuading them to continue trusting in God's grace. *(EXB)* ... who talked to them and urged them to continue [to trust themselves to and to stand fast] in the grace (the unmerited favor and blessing) of God. *(AMPC)*

... and the two men urged them to continue to rely on the grace of God. *(NLT)* ... who put before them how important it was to keep on in the grace of God. *(BBE)* ... to remain faithful to the message of God's grace. *(CEB)*

Hebrews 13:7-9

Remember your leaders who taught you the word of God. Think of all the good that has come from their lives, and follow the example of their faith.

Jesus Christ is the same yesterday, today, and forever. So do not be attracted by strange, new ideas. Your strength comes from God's grace, not from rules about food, which don't help those who follow them. *(NLT)*

... Don't be carried away by various and strange teachings, for it is good that the heart be established by grace, not by food ... *(WEB)*

... for it is good for the heart to be established and ennobled and strengthened by means of grace (God's favor and spiritual blessing) ... *(AMPC)* ... for [it is] good that the heart be confirmed with grace ... *(DARBY)*

PRAYING THE WORD OF GRACE

Heavenly Father, I thank You for Your abundant grace, which is the source of my salvation – and my life in Christ – from start to finish. It is by the grace and the Spirit of God, through faith, that I entered into life in Christ, and not by the flesh. And it is by the same grace and Spirit of God, through faith in You, that I finish and continue my journey with You, and complete the good purposes that You have laid out for me to accomplish.

I received Christ Jesus the Lord by grace through faith. I accepted Him, and now by Your Spirit and grace which enables me, I continue to follow Him and walk in Him. Father, I thank You for placing me in Christ. I ask You to renew my mind and thinking, and reveal to me the wonder of the union I have in Him, that I may conduct myself as one with Him, building my life upon Christ, in step with Him, and transformed into Your way of being.

Thank You for firmly planting me in Christ. I allow my roots to go down deep, fixed and founded in Christ, and I allow You to continually build me up in Him. In Your Spirit and grace, I am becoming increasingly more confirmed and established in my faith. Father, teach me how to partner with You, and surrender to Your instruction, that my faith would grow strong in the truth I was taught. My heart overflows with thankfulness for Your caring leadership, and the growth that I get to experience, out of the fullness of Your grace and truth!

Witnessing your grace and favor in action causes ecstatic rejoicing! Your grace is so amazing! Father, I hear the heartfelt encouragement, sincere exhortation, and even urgent warning of Your servants in Scripture, to cleave unto and remain devoted to the Lord Jesus and Your grace. Father, I ask that You increase in me a resolute and steady purpose of heart, to remain true to You, and faithful to the word of Your grace. Show me how to not just trust in Your grace at the start of my faith journey, but all throughout.

So, I continue in the grace of God. I continue to rely on Your grace, Father, through Jesus Christ. I daily trust myself to, abide and stand fast in Your grace, favor and blessing, which I received apart from any merit. In Your strength, I remain faithful to Your message of grace.

I remember the leaders who taught me the word of God, along with the apostles of Jesus Christ who wrote the message down by the Spirit of God. I think of their radical faith, how they were called by Your grace, and gave themselves to Your gospel. I meditate on all the good that came from their lives. Jesus Christ is the same yesterday, today, and forever. The message of grace is pure and true, and will never change. My strength comes from Your grace, not by following rules about food, or other strange teachings which try to add to Your word.

Father, keep my heart pure and guarded from strange, new ideas. It is good for my heart to be established by grace. Yes, my heart is ennobled and strengthened and confirmed by means of Your grace, by Your Spirit, and Your favor and spiritual blessing.

I thank You that You give me the power by the Holy Spirit to continue following the Lord in grace. Grant me the wisdom to discern teachings that come my way, that I may stay on Your path, which I entered into by the grace of God. Strengthen me in Christ, and deeply root my faith in Him, giving me a bold confidence in Your grace. It is through Him, and by faith in His name that I pray, Amen!

11

GRACE WHICH STRENGTHENS ME IN TRIALS

1 Peter 5:10, 2 Corinthians 12:9, 2 Thessalonians 2:16-17, Philippians 4:13, 2 Timothy 2:1

1 Peter 5:10

The God of all grace, who called you to his eternal glory in Christ, will himself restore, establish, strengthen, and support you after you have suffered a little while. *(CSB)*

And after you suffer for a short time [or a little], God, who gives all grace, will make everything right [restore you]. He will make you strong and support you and keep you from falling. He called you to share in his glory in Christ, a glory that will continue forever [into his eternal glory in Christ]. *(EXB)*

... the God of all grace [Who imparts all blessing and favor], Who has called you to His [own] eternal glory in Christ Jesus, will Himself complete and make you what you ought to be, establish and ground you securely, and strengthen, and settle you. *(AMPC)* ... and make you strong, firm and steadfast. *(NIV)*

John 16:33

"I have told you these things, so that in me you may have peace. In this world you will have trouble. But take heart! I have overcome the world." *(NIV)*

I have told you these things, so that in Me you may have [perfect] peace and confidence. In the world you have tribulation and trials and distress and frustration; but be of good cheer [take courage; be confident, certain, undaunted]! For I have overcome the world. [I have deprived it of power to harm you and have conquered it for you.] *(AMPC)*

... In the world you have distress. But be encouraged! I have conquered the world. *(CEB)*

... but be courageous [be confident, be undaunted, be filled with joy]; I have overcome the world." [My conquest is accomplished, My victory abiding.] *(AMP)*

2 Corinthians 12:9

But he said to me, "My grace is sufficient for you, for my power is made perfect in weakness." Therefore I will boast all the more gladly of my weaknesses, so that the power of Christ may rest upon me. *(ESV)* ... so that the power of Christ may dwell in me. *(NASB)* ... so that the power of Christ can work through me. *(NLT)*

But He said to me, My grace (My favor and loving-kindness and mercy) is enough for you [sufficient against any danger and enables you to bear the trouble manfully]; for My strength and power are made perfect (fulfilled and completed) and show themselves most effective in [your] weakness. Therefore, I will all the more gladly glory in my weaknesses and infirmities, that the strength and power of Christ (the Messiah) may rest (yes, may pitch a tent over and dwell) upon me! *(AMPC)*

2 Thessalonians 2:16-17

Now may our Lord Jesus Christ Himself, and our God and Father, who has loved us and given us everlasting consolation and good hope by grace, comfort your hearts and establish you in every good word and work. *(NKJV)*

May our Lord Jesus Christ himself and God our Father, who loved us and through his grace gave us eternal comfort [encouragement] and a good hope, encourage [comfort] you and strengthen you in every good thing you do and say. *(EXB)*

... May he encourage your hearts and ... *(CEB)* [make them steadfast and keep them unswerving] in every good work and word. *(AMPC)*

Philippians 4:13

I can do all things through Christ who strengthens me. *(NKJV)*

I can endure all these things through the power of the one who gives me strength. *(CEB)*

I can do all things [which He has called me to do] through Him who strengthens and empowers me [to fulfill His purpose—I am self-sufficient in Christ's sufficiency; I am ready for anything and equal to anything through Him who infuses me with inner strength and confident peace.] *(AMP)*

2 Timothy 2:1

So, my child, draw your strength from the grace that is in Christ Jesus. *(CEB)*

So you, my son, be strong [constantly strengthened] and empowered in the grace that is [to be found only] in Christ Jesus. *(AMP)*

Praying the Word of Grace

Heavenly Father, You are the God of all grace, who imparts all blessing and favor! You have called me to Your own eternal glory in Christ Jesus, to share in this glory that will continue forever!

When times of trouble come, help me to remember the words of Jesus Christ, which He spoke to us so that in Him, we may have perfect peace and confidence. In this world I will encounter trouble. Yes, this world comes with having tribulation, trials, distress and frustration at times. But I thank You, Father, that there is a greater reality in Christ!

Yes, I know I can take heart, for Christ has overcome the world. Jesus, You have deprived the world of power to harm me, and You have conquered the world for me. Your conquest is accomplished! Your victory is abiding! Therefore, I take courage, and I let myself fill up with good cheer. In Christ's glorious, eternal victory, I am encouraged, confident, certain, and undaunted. I am courageous! I am filled with joy!

Suffering may come, but I thank You, Perfect Father, that after a short time, You will Yourself complete me. You establish me and ground me securely. You strengthen and settle me. You support me and keep me from falling. You make me what I ought to be. You make me strong, firm and steadfast. You make everything right and restore me. How great and marvelous You are!

Father, I thank You, for Your grace is sufficient for me. Your strength and power are made perfect, fulfilled and completed, and show themselves most effective in my weakness. Your grace, favor, loving-kindness and mercy are enough for me. They are sufficient against any danger, and they enable me to bear any trouble manfully. Your grace completes me.

So I boast all the more gladly of my weaknesses and human limitations, so that the strength and power of Christ may rest upon me, dwell within me, and can work through me mightily!

I can endure anything, and do all things which You have called me to do, through Christ who gives me strength. Jesus, You empower me to fulfill Your purpose, by the life-giving power of the Holy Spirit! I am self-sufficient in Christ's sufficiency. I am ready for anything, and equal to anything through Christ, who infuses me with inner strength and confident peace. I draw my strength from the grace that is found only in You, Jesus. Yes, Lord Jesus, I am constantly strengthened in Your grace.

I surrender my life to You, Lord Jesus! I open my innermost being to You, Holy Spirit! I give You my heart, my God and my Father, for You have loved me and given me everlasting consolation, and good hope, by Your grace!

I am confident that You Yourself will now comfort my heart and establish me in every good word and work. I ask, Father, by the power of Your grace and Spirit, in everything I do and say, for You to encourage my heart, strengthen me, make me steadfast and keep me unswerving. By the glorious grace of Jesus Christ, and in His name, I pray. Amen!

12

FINDING HIS AMAZING GRACE TO HELP IN TIME OF NEED

*Hebrews 4:15-16, James 4:6, Psalm 51:1,
Lamentations 3:22-23, Psalm 13:5, 1 John 4:16,
1 Corinthians 13:4-8*

Hebrews 4:15-16

... Let us then with confidence draw near to the throne of grace, that we may receive mercy and find grace to help in time of need. *(ESV)*

... We may come near, then, with freedom, to the throne of the grace, that we may receive kindness, and find grace — for seasonable help. *(YLT)*

For we do not have a High Priest who is unable to sympathize and understand our weaknesses and temptations, but One who has been tempted [knowing exactly how it feels to be human] in every respect as we are, yet without [committing any] sin.

Therefore let us [with privilege] approach the throne of grace [that is, the throne of God's gracious favor] with confidence and without fear, so that we may receive mercy [for our failures] and find [His amazing] grace to help in

time of need [an appropriate blessing, coming just at the right moment].
(AMP)

... So let us come boldly to the throne of our gracious God. There we will receive his mercy, and we will find grace to help us when we need it most. *(NLT)*

James 4:6

But He gives more grace. Therefore He says: "God resists the proud, but gives grace to the humble." *(NKJV)*

... but gives grace [continually] to the lowly (those who are humble enough to receive it). *(AMPC)*

But He gives us more and more grace [through the power of the Holy Spirit to defy sin and live an obedient life that reflects both our faith and our gratitude for our salvation]. Therefore, it says, "God is opposed to the proud and haughty, but [continually] gives [the gift of] grace to the humble [who turn away from self-righteousness]." *(AMP)*

Psalm 51:1

Be gracious to me, God,
according to Your faithful love;
according to Your abundant compassion,
blot out my rebellion. *(HCSB)*

... out of a full heart, take away my sin. *(BBE)*

Lamentations 3:22-23

The steadfast love of the Lord never ceases;
his mercies never come to an end;
they are new every morning;
great is your faithfulness. *(ESV)*

... his mercies begin afresh each morning. *(NLT)*

... His [tender] compassions fail not. They are new every morning; great and abundant is Your stability and faithfulness. *(AMPC)*

Psalm 13:5

But I have trusted in Your faithful love; my heart will rejoice in Your deliverance. *(HCSB)*

But I trust in your unfailing love. I will rejoice because you have rescued me. *(NLT)*

But I have trusted, leaned on, and been confident in Your mercy and lovingkindness; my heart shall rejoice and be in high spirits in Your salvation. *(AMPC)*

I trust [have confidence] in your love [loyalty; covenant love]. My heart is happy [rejoices] because you saved me [of your victory/salvation]. *(EXB)*

1 John 4:16

And we have known and believed the love that God has for us. God is love, and he who abides in love abides in God, and God in him. *(NKJV)*

And we know (understand, recognize, are conscious of, by observation and by experience) and believe (adhere to and put faith in and rely on) the love God cherishes for us. God is love, and he who dwells and continues in love dwells and continues in God, and God dwells and continues in him. *(AMPC)*

We know how much God loves us, and we have put our trust in his love. God is love, and all who live in love live in God, and God lives in them. *(NLT)*

... God is love, and the one who remains in love remains in God ... *(NASB)*

1 Corinthians 13:4-8

Love is patient, love is kind. It does not envy, it does not boast, it is not proud. It does not dishonor others, it is not self-seeking, it is not easily angered, it keeps no record of wrongs. Love does not delight in evil but rejoices with the truth. It always protects, always trusts, always hopes, always perseveres.

Love never fails... *(NIV)*

Love endures with patience and serenity, love is kind and thoughtful, and is not jealous or envious; love does not brag and is not proud or arrogant. It is not rude; it is not self-seeking, it is not provoked [nor overly sensitive and easily angered]; it does not take into account a wrong endured. It does not rejoice at injustice, but rejoices with the truth [when right and truth prevail]. Love bears all things [regardless of what comes], believes all things [looking for the best in each one], hopes all things [remaining steadfast during difficult times], endures all things [without weakening].

Love never fails [it never fades nor ends]... *(AMP)*

Praying the Word of Grace

Oh Merciful Creator and Heavenly Father! How abundant is Your grace; how steadfast is Your love! Your tender compassions fail not, they never cease! Your mercies never come to an end! They are new every morning. Yes, Your mercies begin afresh each day. Great and abundant is Your stability, and Your faithfulness.

I trust in Your unfailing, faithful love. I am confident in Your mercy and loving-kindness, in Your loyalty and Your covenant love. So, Abba Father, I lean on You, and fall into Your arms, giving You all my weight and my complete trust. My heart is so happy because You have saved me! My heart shall rejoice and be in the highest spirits because of Your salvation and deliverance. You have won it all for me! Yes, Jesus, You have the victory!

Father, I thank You with a humble heart. I did nothing to deserve all of this, but You are gracious to me, according to Your faithful love. According to Your abundant compassion, You have blotted out my rebellion. Out of a full heart, You take away my sin.

You love me so much, Father. You cherish and adore me. I have known and experienced, and I put my trust in Your love. And I see, Father, that You Yourself are love. As I abide in Your love, I abide in You, and You abide in me. I live in love, I live in God, and God lives in me. What an astounding reality.

You are love, and love is patient and kind. This means that You, Father, are patient and kind by nature. Father, I thank You that You endure, with patience and serenity. You are kind and thoughtful. You are not easily angered, and You keep no record of wrongs. My record of wrongs was nailed to the cross of Christ! You do not rejoice at injustice, but You rejoice with the truth. And I rejoice with You, the truth of Christ sets me free: from sin and all its effects!

You always protect, and You bear all things. You believe all things, and look for the best in each of Your children. You always hope and remain steadfast in difficult times. You always persevere, enduring all things without weakening. Father, You never fail. You and Your love never fade or end. How wonderful it is to rest in the truth of Your unfailing love, Your abundant grace, and Your pure heart. How blissful it is to rest in You!

Jesus, Son of God, You have the victory! You have passed through the heavens, and have finished the work of redemption on my behalf. You also fully lived the human life, so You know exactly how it feels to be tempted in every way, and You are able to sympathize with our weaknesses. Yet, You were without sin. Jesus, our High Priest, how holy and beautiful You are! How gracious and understanding! You are the Way, the Truth, and the Life!

I thank You that I may draw near to You with confidence. What privilege You have bestowed upon me! I may come boldly with freedom, and without fear, to the throne of grace. I ask You, by the Holy Spirit, that You remind me of this precious truth constantly, so that I may come freely, to receive kindness and mercy, and to find Your amazing grace to help in time of need. There, I may always find the appropriate blessing, coming at just the right moment, and grace to help me when I need it most.

And You always give more grace! How breathtakingly powerful this is! Father, true humility is found in fully accepting Your gift, and not being too proud to receive, or trying to prove our own worth by attempting to merit your grace through self-righteousness. I turn away from all self-righteousness. You give grace because it's who You are. In Christ, You have given it all. I turn away from pride, and confess boldly: it is not by my works or merit that I can come to Your throne of grace. It is purely through Your Beloved Son, in whom I have trusted!

You give the gift of grace continually to the humble, to those who know they need grace. I know that I need Your grace, and I know You give it in abundance. So I receive it now, even more abundantly! You give more and more grace, every moment without ceasing, through the power of the Holy Spirit. Your unending grace empowers me to defy sin and live an obedient life that reflects my faith and gratitude for salvation. You empower me by Your grace to live the new life in Christ!

If there is any way, Father, that I have believed Your grace is limited, or that I have to earn it... if there is any way I have been leaning on my own self-right-eousness, or have forgotten the joy of my salvation in Christ... if there is any way I am not experiencing the boldness to come before Your throne of grace which You have given me freely, if I am afraid to ask You for help or mercy when I need it most... I ask for You to reveal these places in my heart, and heal my understanding, so that I may walk in the fullness of life in Christ Jesus, by Your amazing grace. I boldly pray all this in the name of Jesus, Amen!

13

FREEDOM FROM SIN BY THE GRACE OF GOD

Romans 6:14, Titus 2:11-12, Jude 1:24-25, 1 John 2:1-2, Micah 7:19, Hebrews 8:12, 1 Peter 2:24, Romans 6:2, Hebrews 12:1-2, Philippians 3:12-16

Romans 6:14

For sin shall not have dominion over you, for you are not under law but under grace. *(NKJV)*

Sin is no longer your master, for you no longer live under the requirements of the law. Instead, you live under the freedom of God's grace. *(NLT)*

For sin will no longer be a master over you, since you are not under Law [as slaves], but under [unmerited] grace [as recipients of God's favor and mercy]. *(AMP)*

For sin will not rule over you ... *(CSB)*

Titus 2:11-12

For the grace of God has appeared, bringing salvation for all people, training us to renounce ungodliness and worldly passions, and to live self-controlled, upright, and godly lives in the present age. *(ESV)*

For the grace of God has appeared that offers salvation to all people. It teaches us to say "No" to ungodliness and worldly passions ... *(NIV)* ... It educates us so that we can live sensible, ethical, and godly lives right now ... *(CEB)* ... We should live in this evil world with wisdom, righteousness, and devotion to God. *(NLT)*

... It teaches [trains; disciplines] us to turn away from [reject; deny] ungodly living and the evil things the world wants to do [or worldly desires; sinful pleasures]. Instead, that grace teaches us to live in the present age in a wise [self-controlled] and right [upright; just] way and in a way that shows we serve God [godly manner]. *(EXB)*

... It has trained us to reject and renounce all ungodliness (irreligion) and worldly (passionate) desires, to live discreet (temperate, self-controlled), upright, devout (spiritually whole) lives in this present world. *(AMPC)*

Jude 1:24-25

Now to Him who is able to keep you from stumbling, And to present you faultless Before the presence of His glory with exceeding joy, To God our Savior, Who alone is wise, Be glory and majesty, Dominion and power, Both now and forever. Amen. *(NKJV)*

Now to him who is able to keep you from falling, and to give you a place in his glory, free from all evil, with great joy ... *(BBE)*

Now to Him Who is able to keep you without stumbling or slipping or falling, and to present [you] unblemished (blameless and faultless) before the presence of His glory in triumphant joy and exultation [with unspeakable, ecstatic delight] ... *(AMPC)*

1 John 2:1-2

My dear children, I write this to you so that you will not sin. But if anybody does sin, we have an advocate with the Father—Jesus Christ, the Righteous One. He is the atoning sacrifice for our sins, and not only for ours but also for the sins of the whole world. *(NIV)*

Micah 7:19

He will again have compassion on us; he will tread our iniquities underfoot. You will cast all our sins into the depths of the sea. *(ESV)*

… He will vanquish our iniquities … *(HCSB)* … He will subdue and tread underfoot our wickedness [destroying sin's power] … *(AMP)*

… and you will send all our sins down into the heart of the sea. *(BBE)*

You will have mercy [compassion] on us again; you will conquer our sins. You will throw away [hurl; cast] all our sins into the deepest part [depths] of the sea. *(EXB)*

Hebrews 8:12

"For I will be merciful and gracious toward their wickedness,
And I will remember their sins no more." *(AMP)*

And I will forgive their wickedness,
and I will never again remember their sins. *(NLT)*

1 Peter 2:24

He personally carried our sins in His body on the cross [willingly offering Himself on it, as on an altar of sacrifice], so that we might die to sin [becoming immune from the penalty and power of sin] and live for righteousness; for by His wounds you [who believe] have been healed. *(AMP)*

Romans 6:2

... We are those who have died to sin; how can we live in it any longer? *(NIV)*

Hebrews 12:1-2

Therefore, since we are surrounded by such a huge crowd of witnesses to the life of faith, let us strip off every weight that slows us down, especially the sin that so easily trips us up. And let us run with endurance the race God has set before us. We do this by keeping our eyes on Jesus, the champion who initiates and perfects our faith. Because of the joy awaiting him, he endured the cross, disregarding its shame. Now he is seated in the place of honor beside God's throne. *(NLT)*

Therefore, since we are surrounded by so great a cloud of witnesses [who by faith have testified to the truth of God's absolute faithfulness] ... *(AMP)*

... let us strip off and throw aside every encumbrance (unnecessary weight) and that sin which so readily (deftly and cleverly) clings to and entangles us, and let us run with patient endurance and steady and active persistence the appointed course of the race that is set before us,

Looking away [from all that will distract] to Jesus, Who is the Leader and the Source of our faith [giving the first incentive for our belief] and is also its Finisher [bringing it to maturity and perfection]. He, for the joy [of obtaining the prize] that was set before Him, endured the cross, despising and ignoring the shame, and is now seated at the right hand of the throne of God. *(AMPC)*

Philippians 3:12-16

Not that I have already obtained all this, or have already arrived at my goal, but I press on to take hold of that for which Christ Jesus took hold of me. Brothers and sisters, I do not consider myself yet to have taken hold of it. But one thing I do: Forgetting what is behind and straining toward what is ahead, I press on toward the goal to win the prize for which God has called me heavenward in Christ Jesus.

All of us, then, who are mature should take such a view of things. And if on some point you think differently, that too God will make clear to you. Only let us live up to what we have already attained. *(NIV)*

Praying the Word of Grace

Invincible Heavenly Father, You have won the complete victory over sin! I thank You for Your uncontainable compassion You have for us; Your unlimited mercy and grace that You have poured upon us over and again; and Your unstoppable power with which You defeated sin, death and the enemy of our souls!

Through Christ, and His finished work, You conquered our sins, and You tread them underfoot. You subdued our wickedness. You vanquished our iniquity. You destroyed sin's power for good. Almighty God, You are unmatched! All glory to God and His triumphant, amazing grace through Jesus Christ!

I thank You, Father, for You have thrown all our sins into the deepest parts of the sea. You have sent them down into the depths forever. Jesus personally carried all our sins in His body on the Cross, willingly offering Himself on it, as on an altar of sacrifice. He did this so we would die to sin and live for righteousness.

In You, Jesus, I enter into a supernatural immunity from the penalty and power of sin. I believe in Your matchless power, which works mightily in me by the Holy Spirit. I ask to be more deeply grounded in Your Heavenly reality, so that I may experience it more fully in my life here on earth! By Your wounds, I have truly been healed!

In You, Jesus, sin is no longer my master, for I no longer live under the requirements of the law as a slave. Instead, I live under the freedom of Your grace! As a recipient of Your free unmerited favor, Your mercy, Your glorious grace, and empowering Holy Spirit: sin will not rule over me, nor any longer have any dominion over me. I have died to sin! How could I live any longer in it? I am saved and set free, and now, I live unto righteousness through the free gift of grace!

For the grace of God has appeared, bringing salvation for all people. Grace disciplines me to reject and renounce all ungodliness, worldly passions and desires, and sinful pleasures. Grace teaches me to turn away from ungodly living, and to say "no" to the evil things the world wants to do. Grace trains me, so that in this present age, I am equipped to live a life that is wise, self-controlled, sensible, upright, just, devout, godly, and spiritually whole. Grace enables me to live with wisdom, righteousness, and devotion to God; and to live in a way that shows I serve the God of grace, with passion and delight!

Thank You, Father, for placing me in Christ. In Him, through the power of the Holy Spirit, You are able to keep me from stumbling, slipping or falling. What a marvelous truth! You are able to present me faultless, unblemished and blameless before the presence of Your glory in triumphant joy and exultation. You are able to give me a place in Your glory, free from all evil. In Your glory, I am filled with perfect peace, and unspeakable, ecstatic delight!

With man this may be impossible; but I thank You, Father, that with You, all things are possible! You paid dearly so that I could live victorious and transformed, living a whole new life in Christ! In Him, You've given me all I need! It is not by my might nor power, but by Your all-sufficient grace and the power of the Holy Spirit.

You are always faithful, and have always been faithful. I am surrounded by such a great cloud of witnesses, who, by faith, have testified to the truth of Your absolute faithfulness. The testimony of Your faithfulness echoes through all time! This is who You are!

If there is anything I am holding onto which gets in the way of experiencing Heaven's reality, Father, I pray that You would reveal this to me, so that I may cast it aside, and run my race without hindrance. Help me to realize – with joy, peace, freedom and clarity – that any sin is just unnecessary weight that only entangles and slows me down. Teach me to throw aside all distractions and superfluous weight, Holy Spirit. I believe that in Christ, You have set me free already, so I pray for Your freedom to fully manifest in my life, here and now.

Jesus, I press on to take hold of that for which You took hold of me. Help me to forget what is behind me. You remember my sins no more, so help me to let go, forget them, and forgive as You have forgiven, in the overflow Your mercy and grace! Jesus, You took sin, along with all its shame and guilt, onto the Cross with You. So I surrender all sin, guilt and shame to You, Jesus.

If I do stumble along the way, Lord Jesus, I have You as my advocate in the presence of the Father, and You restore me to my feet. You are the Righteous

One, and the atoning sacrifice for our sins. You died to take away not only my sins, but also the sins of the whole world!

So, Father, in the freedom and strength of Your grace through Jesus, may I leave what is behind, and run toward what is ahead. I receive Your insight and grace to make things right that I need to make right, and to wholeheartedly live the holy life for which You've chosen me! I fully embrace You Jesus, for You have fully embraced me!

Father, I press on toward the joy set before me, toward the Heavenly prize to which You have called me in Christ Jesus! If in any way I am thinking in a different way, I thank You that You will make that clear to me, and empower me to live in the fullness of grace and truth.

I thank You, Jesus, my Champion, for the supernatural strength that fills me as I fix my eyes on You. You are my vision and focus, as I run with patient endurance, and active and steady persistence, on the appointed course that is set before me. You are the Champion who both initiates and perfects my faith. You are the source of my faith, giving the first incentive for my belief. At the same time, You are also its finisher, bringing it to maturity and perfection.

And You saw the great joy set before You, and You endured the Cross, despising and ignoring its shame. Now You are seated in honor, at the right hand of God! I run my race, empowered by and inspired by the victory You already won!

To God my Savior, who alone is wise, be glory and majesty, dominion and power, both now and forever! I give all my praise to God the Father, the Holy Spirit, and Jesus Christ! By Your infinite power, through Your finished work, You have conquered sin and death on my behalf, and given me the victory by means of Your grace. In Christ's all-powerful name, Amen!

14

BORN AGAIN INTO A NEW LIFE

Ephesians 2:4-5, Romans 6:3-4, Colossians 3:3,
1 Peter 1:23, 2 Corinthians 5:17

Ephesians 2:4-5

But God, who is rich in mercy, because of His great love with which He loved us, even when we were dead in trespasses, made us alive together with Christ (by grace you have been saved) *(NKJV)*

But God—so rich is He in His mercy! Because of and in order to satisfy the great and wonderful and intense love with which He loved us, Even when we were dead (slain) by [our own] shortcomings and trespasses, He made us alive together in fellowship and in union with Christ; [He gave us the very life of Christ Himself, the same new life with which He quickened Him, for] it is by grace (His favor and mercy which you did not deserve) that you are saved (delivered from judgment and made partakers of Christ's salvation). *(AMPC)*

... he gave us life when he raised Christ from the dead ... *(NLT)*

Romans 6:3-4

Or do you not know that all of us who have been baptized into Christ Jesus have been baptized into His death? Therefore we have been buried with Him through baptism into death, so that, just as Christ was raised from the dead through the glory of the Father, so we too may walk in newness of life. *(ESV)*

... When we were baptized, we were buried with Christ and shared his [and participated in his; into] death. So, just as Christ was raised from the dead by the wonderful power [glorious power; glory] of the Father, we also can live a new life. *(EXB)*

Colossians 3:3

For you died, and your life is hidden with Christ in God. *(NKJV)*

For you died [to this world], and your [new, real] life is hidden with Christ in God. *(AMP)*

For your life on earth is done, and you have a secret life with Christ in God. *(BBE)*

1 Peter 1:23

For you have been born again, not of perishable seed, but of imperishable, through the living and enduring word of God. *(NIV)*

For you have been born again [that is, reborn from above—spiritually transformed, renewed, and set apart for His purpose] not of seed which is perishable but [from that which is] imperishable and immortal, that is, through the living and everlasting word of God. *(AMP)*

2 Corinthians 5:17

Therefore, if anyone is in Christ, he is a new creation; old things have passed away; behold, all things have become new. *(NKJV)*

Therefore if anyone is in Christ [that is, grafted in, joined to Him by faith in Him as Savior], he is a new creature [reborn and renewed by the Holy Spirit]; the old things [the previous moral and spiritual condition] have passed away. Behold, new things have come [because spiritual awakening brings a new life]. *(AMP)*

This means that anyone who belongs to Christ has become a new person. The old life is gone; a new life has begun! *(NLT)* ... he is in a new world: the old things have come to an end; they have truly become new. *(BBE)* ... look, new things have arrived! *(CEB)*

Praying the Word of Grace

Wonderful and Gracious Heavenly Father! You are so rich in mercy! You have loved us with such a great love; a wonderful and intense love! Because of Your love, and in order to satisfy Your love, You made me alive together in fellowship in fellowship and in union with Christ. You have done in me what would have been impossible without You.

You raised me from the dead, Father. Oh, the miracle and wonder of it! Even when I was dead in trespasses, slain by my own shortcomings, You made me alive together with Christ. You gave me the very life of Christ Himself, and I am raised with Him. You gave me the same new life with which You quickened Jesus, the resurrection life that brought Him out from the grave. What a glorious mystery!

You saved me by Your grace, favor and mercy, which I did nothing to deserve. You delivered me from judgment and made me a partaker of Christ's salvation. I have been united, grafted together with Christ by grace, through faith in Him. Through baptism, I was buried with Him and participated in His death. In Him, I died to this world. My old life on earth is done.

And just as Christ was raised from the dead through the glory and wonderful power of the Father, I also may walk in newness of life. I have a new life to live in Christ! My new, real life is hidden with Christ in God. It's a secret life, and in order to unveil it, I set my mind on things above, where Christ is. I ask You, Father, to reveal my new life to me.

Father I thank You that in Christ, I have been born again! I have been reborn from above, spiritually transformed, renewed, and set apart for Your purpose. I was born again, not of seed which is perishable, but from that which is imperishable and immortal: through the living, enduring and everlasting word of God!

You have said that anyone who belongs to Christ has become a new person. I am grafted in, joined to Him by trusting in Him as my Savior. I thank You that in Christ, I am an entirely new kind of creation. I am reborn and renewed by the Holy Spirit! The old things have passed away, all of the previous moral and spiritual condition is over. All things have become new, because this spiritual awakening brings an entirely new life.

I look up with the wonder of a child, and behold with gratitude, that I am in a new world. All the old things have come to an end. Look, new things have arrived! The old life is gone: a new life has begun. Father, I thank You that "all things" means that everything has, in fact, truly become brand new. Regardless of the natural world around me, there is a new world I have entered into by the Spirit. May I walk according to the Spirit!

Father, would You open my eyes to this glorious new life? Make me know the power of Christ and His resurrection, to which I've been united. Cause me to experience the mighty working of the Holy Spirit's power, with whom You have filled me, and by whom You raised Christ from the dead. And help me to grow in this magnificent grace by which You've saved me, that I may walk fully and completely in the newness of life. In Christ's name, I pray, Amen!

15

CALLED BY THE GRACE OF GOD

2 Timothy 1:9, Galatians 1:15-16, Romans 1:5, Ephesians 2:10, John 10:10, 1 Corinthians 1:9

2 Timothy 1:9

God is the one who saved and called us with a holy calling. This wasn't based on what we have done, but it was based on his own purpose and grace that he gave us in Christ Jesus before time began. *(CEB)*

... He delivered us and saved us and called us with a holy calling [a calling that leads to a consecrated life—a life set apart—a life of purpose], not because of our works [or because of any personal merit—we could do nothing to earn this], but because of His own purpose and grace [His amazing, undeserved favor] which was granted to us in Christ Jesus before the world began [eternal ages ago] *(AMP)*

Romans 1:5

We have received grace and apostleship through Him to bring about the obedience of faith among all the nations, on behalf of His name. *(HCSB)*

Through whom grace has been given to us, sending us out to make disciples to the faith among all nations, for his name. *(BBE)*

Galatians 1:15-16

But even before I was born, God chose me and called me by his marvelous grace ... *(NLT)*

But when God, who from my mother's womb set me apart and called me by his grace, was pleased to reveal his Son in me, so that I could preach him among the Gentiles, I did not immediately consult with anyone. *(CSB)*

But when He, Who had chosen and set me apart [even] before I was born and had called me by His grace (His undeserved favor and blessing), saw fit and was pleased to reveal (unveil, disclose) His Son within me ... *(AMPC)*

But when it was the good pleasure of God, by whom I was marked out even from my mother's body, through his grace, to give the revelation of his Son in me ... *(BBE)* ... that I may announce him as glad tidings among the nations ... *(DARBY)*

Ephesians 2:10

For we are God's masterpiece. He has created us anew in Christ Jesus, so we can do the good things he planned for us long ago. *(NLT)*

For we are His workmanship [His own master work, a work of art], created in Christ Jesus [reborn from above—spiritually transformed, renewed, ready to be used] for good works, which God prepared [for us] beforehand [taking paths which He set], so that we would walk in them [living the good life which He prearranged and made ready for us]. *(AMP)*

John 10:10

The thief comes only to steal and kill and destroy; I have come that they may have life, and have it to the full. *(NIV)*

The thief's purpose is to steal and kill and destroy. My purpose is to give them a rich and satisfying life. *(NLT)*

The thief enters only to steal, kill, and destroy. I came so that they could have life—indeed, so that they could live life to the fullest. *(CEB)*

... I have come that they may have life, and that they may have it more abundantly. *(NKJV)* ... and have it in greater measure. *(BBE)*

... I came that they may have and enjoy life, and have it in abundance [to the full, till it overflows]. *(AMP)*

... I came to give life [that they might have life]—life in all its fullness [abundance]. *(EXB)*

1 Corinthians 1:9

God is faithful, through whom you were called into the fellowship of his Son, Jesus Christ, our Lord. *(WEB)*

God is faithful (reliable, trustworthy, and therefore ever true to His promise, and He can be depended on); by Him you were called into companionship and participation with His Son, Jesus Christ our Lord. *(AMPC)*

Praying the Word of Grace

Father of all Goodness, You are the Magnificent One who saved me and called me with a holy calling. I am overtaken with ecstasy, knowing that even before I was born, You chose me and called me by Your marvelous grace! By Your grace, and Your undeserved favor and blessing, You marked me from my mother's womb. You set me part unto a consecrated life, a life of purpose. Oh how glorious, Father! You've always had a plan for me!

Your holy calling for me was not based on anything I had done, or because of any personal merit. I could do nothing to earn this. It was based on Your own purpose and grace, and Your amazing undeserved favor, which You gave us in Christ Jesus before the world and time began.

I am bursting with gratitude, Father! For it was Your good pleasure, through Your grace, to reveal and unveil Your Son within me. Through Your Son, I have received grace to be sent out to accomplish my God-given purpose in life. By Your grace, I am empowered to announce Him as glad tidings among the nations, bringing the light of His faith to the world, on behalf of His precious name: to unveil Your Son as You have with me!

Father, thank You for creating me! And thank You for re-creating me anew in Christ Jesus! I have been reborn from above, spiritually transformed and renewed, and ready to be used for Your glory and purpose. You saved me and called me by Your grace, for a masterful purpose, so I could do the things You planned for me long ago.

Thank You for the wonderful intentions You had for me from before I was born, even before time began. I am Your workmanship, Your own work of art. I am the very masterpiece of God, created anew in Christ Jesus for good works. Father, I trust in You as I take the paths which You set for me to walk in, living the good life which You prearranged and made ready for me.

Jesus, I thank You for the abundant life You have given, and continually give to me! You came so that we may have and enjoy a rich and satisfying life, living out Your marvelous plans and gracious good will. I open my arms to receive what You came to give, Your life in greater measure, till it overflows! May I live out the glorious purpose You designed especially for me, and may the thief be kept far from my life and purpose. I surrender to Your plans and Your grace, Jesus, that may live life to the fullest, in all its abundance, fully alive in You!

Jesus, I get to live in full companionship and fellowship with You. How phenomenal! Father, You are so faithful. You are reliable and trustworthy, and therefore ever true to Your promise. You can be depended on! By Your faithfulness, and by Your grace, I was called into fellowship, companionship and participation with Your Son, Jesus Christ our Lord. Thank You for this glorious invitation: I accept with overflowing gratitude!

Thank You for Your calling on my life. I pray that by Your grace, through Your Holy Spirit, You would grant me wisdom and understanding of my particular purpose and calling. Unveil Your Son within me, in glorious new ways, and with ever-increasing clarity and assurance. Reveal to me my participation with Jesus. Allow me to experience the fullness of life, in intimate fellowship and companionship with You, Father, and Your Beloved Son Jesus, and the Holy Spirit. I ask for these things in the name of Jesus Christ, Our Lord, Amen!

16

BY THE GRACE OF GOD I AM WHAT I AM

*1 Corinthians 15:10, 1 Corinthians 1:30-31,
Philippians 2:13, 2 Corinthians 3:5*

1 Corinthians 15:10

But by the grace of God I am what I am: and his grace which was bestowed upon me was not in vain; but I laboured more abundantly than they all: yet not I, but the grace of God which was with me. *(KJV)*

... But whatever I am now, it is all because God poured out his special favor on me—and not without results ... *(NLT)* ... His grace which was given to me was not futile, but I worked more than all of them ... *(WEB)* ... and God's grace hasn't been for nothing ... *(CEB)* ... and his grace to me was not wasted ... *(EXB)*

But by the grace (the unmerited favor and blessing) of God I am what I am, and His grace toward me was not [found to be] for nothing (fruitless and without effect). In fact, I worked harder than all of them [the apostles], though it was not really I, but the grace (the unmerited favor and blessing) of God which was with me. *(AMPC)*

1 Corinthians 1:30-31

But of Him you are in Christ Jesus, who became for us wisdom from God—and righteousness and sanctification and redemption—that, as it is written, "He who glories, let him glory in the Lord." *(NKJV)*

But it is from Him that you have your life in Christ Jesus ... *(AMPC)* Because of God you are in [united with; in relationship with] Christ Jesus ... *(EXB)* But it is due to Him that you are in Christ Jesus ... *(NASB)*

God has united you with Christ Jesus. For our benefit God made him to be wisdom itself. Christ made us right with God; he made us pure and holy, and he freed us from sin. Therefore, as the Scriptures say, "If you want to boast, boast only about the Lord." *(NLT)*

Philippians 2:13

For it is God who is working in you, enabling you both to desire and to work out His good purpose. *(HCSB)*

God is the one who enables you both to want and to actually live out his good purposes *(CEB)* ... giving you the desire and the power ... *(NLT)* ... both to will and to do for His good pleasure. *(NKJV)*

For it is [not your strength, but it is] God who is effectively at work in you, both to will and to work [that is, strengthening, energizing, and creating in you the longing and the ability to fulfill your purpose] for His good pleasure. *(AMP)* ... for His good pleasure and satisfaction and delight. *(AMPC)*

2 Corinthians 3:5

Not that we are sufficient of ourselves to think of anything as being from ourselves, but our sufficiency is from God. *(NKJV)*

Not that we are adequate in ourselves so as to consider anything as having come from ourselves, but our adequacy is from God. *(NASB)*

It is not that we think we are qualified to do anything on our own. Our qualification comes from God. *(NLT)*

We are not saying that we can do this work ourselves ... It is God who makes us able to do all that we do. *(EXB)* ... but our competence is from God. *(HCSB)* ... but our power and ability and sufficiency are from God. *(AMPC)*

Praying the Word of Grace

Wise and Wonderful Heavenly Father, I thank You for bestowing Your inexhaustible grace upon me. You are the cause of my rejoicing, the source of my very life, and the reason I am in Christ! It is from You that I have my life in Christ. It is because of You that I am in relationship with Him. You are the one who united me with Him. Therefore, if I have anything to boast about, I boast in You alone. I lift up all the glory to You, magnificent and gracious God!

Father, You are so abundant in grace and love. For my benefit, You have made Christ to be wisdom itself for me, and righteousness and sanctification and redemption. You made me pure and holy, and You have freed me from sin. This is all by Your amazing grace! Whatever I am now, it is all from You, because You poured out Your special favor and grace upon me.

And Your grace toward me is not for nothing. It is not without effect or results. Your grace is never wasted. No, not at all. It always produces fruit. In fact, it invigorates me to work harder than ever, laboring abundantly. Though it is not really I, but Your grace, favor, power and blessing which are with me!

For it is You who is working in me, enabling me both to desire and to work out Your good pleasure. You are the one who gives me both the desire and the power, to will and to work, enabling me both to want and to actually live out Your good purposes. It is not my strength, but it is You effectively at work in me. You are working in me – strengthening, energizing, and creating in me the longing and the ability – to fulfill my purpose in Christ, for Your good pleasure, satisfaction and delight!

I thank You Father for Your indescribable, glorious, and wise ways! You are the one who actually gives me my purpose, the desire to fulfill it, and the power to carry it out. This is all by Your amazing grace!

Yes, by the grace of God I am what I am. It's true, Your grace makes me who I am! I don't consider that I am sufficient of myself, to think of anything as being from myself. I confess before You that, in and of myself, I am not adequate or qualified or competent to carry out the work You've given me to do. But in You, I am. And indeed, I am in You! You are the one who makes me able to do all that I do. My competence, qualification, adequacy, power, ability and sufficiency are from You, and I have all this in abundance!

Wow, what remarkable truths! By Your grace, and in Christ, I am completely adequate, competent, qualified, powerful and able, and self-sufficient in Christ's sufficiency. In Christ, I have all wisdom, righteousness, sanctification, and redemption. I have been set free from sin, and made pure and holy. Your grace is a free gift, and it is also incredibly effective as it works in me. I have what it takes to do the glorious, purposeful work You've given me to do. I have the drive and desire to work for Your delight! I have the power to work more abundantly than anyone in the purpose You've given me!

Thank You Father, for Your all-sufficient grace, through Your Son, Jesus Christ. I ask You to stir up Your good purposes within me; Your delight and desires; Your abilities and strength; so that I may carry out the glorious plans You have for me in Christ. It's in His powerful name I pray, Amen!

17

FULL OF GRACE AND POWER

Acts 4:33, Acts 6:8, Acts 14:3, Acts 4:29-30,
Ephesians 3:7, Romans 8:11

Acts 4:33

And with great power the apostles were giving testimony to the resurrection of the Lord Jesus, and abundant grace was upon them all. *(NASB)*

And with great ability and power the apostles were continuously testifying to the resurrection of the Lord Jesus, and great grace [God's remarkable lovingkindness and favor and goodwill] rested richly upon them all. *(AMP)*

... And God's grace was so powerfully at work in them all *(NIV)* ... and an abundance of grace was at work among them all. *(CEB)*

Acts 6:8

And Stephen, full of grace and power, was doing great wonders and signs among the people. *(ESV)*

Now Stephen, full of grace (divine blessing and favor) and power (strength and ability) worked great wonders and signs (miracles) among the people. *(AMPC)*

Stephen, who stood out among the believers for the way God's grace was at work in his life and for his exceptional endowment with divine power ... *(CEB)*

Acts 14:3

Therefore they spent a long time there speaking boldly with reliance upon the Lord, who was testifying to the word of His grace, granting that signs and wonders be performed by their hands. *(NASB)* ... taking heart in the Lord, who gave witness to the word of his grace by causing signs and wonders to be done by their hands. *(BBE)*

[So; Therefore] Paul and Barnabas [They] stayed in Iconium a long time and spoke bravely [or boldly] for the Lord. He showed [testified; confirmed] that their message [word] about his grace was true by giving them the power to work [miraculous] signs and miracles [wonders]. *(EXB)*

Acts 4:29-30

And now, O Lord, hear their threats, and give us, your servants, great boldness in preaching your word. Stretch out your hand with healing power; may miraculous signs and wonders be done through the name of your holy servant Jesus. *(NLT)*

... enable your servants to speak your word with complete confidence. *(CEB)* ... [full freedom] to declare Your message fearlessly ... *(AMPC)* ... Show us your power [Stretch out your hand] to heal. Give proofs [signs] and make miracles happen [wonders] by the power [name] of Jesus, your holy servant [or child]. *(EXB)*

Ephesians 3:7

I was made a servant of this gospel by the gift of God's grace that was given to me by the working of His power. *(HCSB)*

By God's grace and mighty power, I have been given the privilege of serving him by spreading this Good News. *(NLT)*

Romans 8:11

The Spirit of God, who raised Jesus from the dead, lives in you. And just as God raised Christ Jesus from the dead, he will give life to your mortal bodies by this same Spirit living within you. *(NLT)*

Praying the Word of Grace

All-powerful and all-loving Heavenly Father; God of grace and God of miracles! I thank You that You pour out abundant grace to work among Your people! And as Your gospel is spread, You confirm it through the mighty working and power of Your Holy Spirit! You are absolute perfection and power; and You are perfect love and grace!

By the gift of Your grace, I have been given the privilege and power to serve You by spreading Your Good News, as a messenger and servant of the gospel. I pray that You give me great boldness, and enable me to speak Your word with complete confidence. Empower me with full freedom to declare Your message fearlessly. And grant me Your precise wisdom and discernment on how to bring timely, anointed words of grace, inspired by Your Holy Spirit, just as You've done in times before.

Abundant grace was on the believers at the beginning of the church, ever since You poured out Your Holy Spirit upon us. And just as Jesus Christ is the same yesterday, today, and forever; that same abundant grace is available to us, and rests upon us now! You are the same God that You were back then!

Show us Your mighty power, God, and stretch out Your hand to heal! May miraculous signs and wonders be done through the power and name of Your holy servant, Your Beloved Son, Jesus Christ. As I participate in the sharing of this glorious Good News – with reliance upon the Lord Jesus, taking heart in You – I thank You for bearing witness to the word of Your grace, by the power of the Holy Spirit.

Thank You, Father. You confirm that Your message of grace is true by causing miracles, signs and wonders to be done by the hands of Your messengers.

Father, I pray that my heart and speech would be confident and bold in grace; that my life would reflect Your goodness and grace; and my hands would be used for Your miraculous healing and powerful work.

Stephen was a man full of grace, divine blessing and favor, as well as power, strength and ability. He stood out among the believers for the way Your grace was at work in his life, and for his exceptional endowment with divine power. By Your grace, He did great miracles, signs and wonders among the people. Father I ask that You empower me with Your grace as You did Stephen!

The apostles of the early church were always giving testimony to the resurrection of the Lord Jesus. As they did, an abundance of Your grace was upon them all, and so powerfully at work within them. Father, I pray that Your same great grace would rest upon us and work so powerfully within us now. May Your remarkable loving-kindness, Your favor and goodwill, and Your miracle-working power rest richly upon me, and on Your church now!

Father, I thank You for the resurrection of the Lord Jesus Christ, how He was raised to life forevermore by the power of the Holy Spirit of God. I am filled with gratitude, faith, wonder and awe, that the same Holy Spirit who raised Jesus Christ from the dead also lives in me. And just as You raised Christ from the dead, You will also give life to my mortal body by the same Holy Spirit living within me. And I believe You will give life to those around me by the Holy Spirit. Oh Father, thank You for Your inexpressible gracious Gift!

Holy Father, I ask You to bring these truths to life for me. Cause me to know by experience the power of Your glorious grace, and the resurrection of Christ! Testify to the truth of Your Good News by working Your miracles in my life and in those around me. In the invincible name of Jesus Christ, I pray, Amen!

18

GOOD STEWARDS OF THE MANIFOLD GRACE OF GOD

*1 Peter 4:10, 1 Corinthians 12:4;7, Romans 12:6,
Psalm 104:24, Genesis 1:31, James 1:17, Psalm 40:5,
1 Timothy 4:4, Psalm 139:14*

1 Peter 4:10

As each one has received a gift, minister it to one another, as good stewards of the manifold grace of God. *(NKJV)*

As each of you has received a gift (a particular spiritual talent, a gracious divine endowment), employ it for one another as [befits] good trustees of God's many-sided grace [faithful stewards of the extremely diverse powers and gifts granted to Christians by unmerited favor]. *(AMPC)*

Making distribution among one another of whatever has been given to you, like true servants of the unmeasured grace of God. *(BBE)*

1 Corinthians 12:4;7

Now there are various kinds of gifts, but the same Spirit ... But to each one is given the manifestation of the Spirit for the profit of all. *(WEB)*

Now there are distinctive varieties and distributions of endowments (gifts, extraordinary powers distinguishing certain Christians, due to the power of divine grace operating in their souls by the Holy Spirit) and they vary, but the [Holy] Spirit remains the same. ... to each one is given the manifestation of the [Holy] Spirit [the evidence, the spiritual illumination of the Spirit] for good and profit. *(AMPC)*

Now there are diversities of graces, but the same Spirit *(DRA)* ... A spiritual gift is given to each of us so we can help each other. *(NLT)*

Romans 12:6

We have different gifts, according to the grace given to each of us ... *(NIV)*

In his grace, God has given us different gifts for doing certain things well ... *(NLT)*

Having gifts (faculties, talents, qualities) that differ according to the grace given us, let us use them ... *(AMPC)*

Psalm 104:24

O LORD, how manifold are thy works! In wisdom hast thou made them all: the earth is full of thy riches. *(KJV)*

Lord, you have done so many things!
You made them all so wisely!
The earth is full of your creations! *(CEB)*

O Lord, how many and varied are Your works!
In wisdom You have made them all;
The earth is full of Your riches and Your creatures. *(AMP)*

Genesis 1:31

And God saw everything that he had made, and behold, it was very good *(ESV)*

James 1:17

Every good gift and every perfect gift is from above, coming down from the Father of lights, with whom there is no variation or shadow due to change. *(ESV)*

Every good thing given and every perfect gift is from above; it comes down from the Father of lights [the Creator and Sustainer of the heavens], in whom there is no variation [no rising or setting] or shadow cast by His turning [for He is perfect and never changes]. *(AMP)*

Every good action [or act of giving] and every perfect gift is from God [comes from above]. These good gifts come down from the Creator of the sun, moon, and stars [the father of lights; referring to God's creation of the heavenly bodies ...], who does not change like their shifting shadows. *(EXB)*

Psalm 40:5

Many, LORD my God, are the wonders you have done, the things you planned for us. None can compare with you; were I to speak and tell of your deeds, they would be too many to declare. *(NIV)*

You, Lord my God!
You've done so many things—
your wonderful deeds and your plans for us—
no one can compare with you!
If I were to proclaim and talk about all of them,
they would be too numerous to count! *(CEB)*

Lord my God, you have done many miracles [wonders; great acts].
Your plans for us are many.
If I tried to tell them all,
there would be too many to count ... *(EXB)*

1 Timothy 4:4

For everything created by God is good, and nothing is to be rejected if it is received with thanksgiving *(ESV)*

Since everything God created is good, we should not reject any of it but receive it with thanks. *(NLT)*

Psalm 139:14

I will give thanks to You, because I am awesomely and wonderfully made; Wonderful are Your works, And my soul knows it very well. *(NASB)*

Thank you for making me so wonderfully complex! Your workmanship is marvelous—how well I know it. *(NLT)*

I will praise You because I have been remarkably and wonderfully made... *(HCSB)* ... fearfully and wonderfully made ... *(NKJV)*

I praise [thank] you because you made me in an amazing [awesome] and wonderful way. What you have done is wonderful. I know this very well. *(EXB)*

Praying the Word of Grace

Magnificent Heavenly Father, Lord Jesus Christ, and Powerful Holy Spirit, I thank You! Merciful Creator of the Heavens and earth: just looking around at Your creation, it is easy to see how indescribably beautiful and creative You are. I marvel at the awesomeness and intelligence of Your design!

Father, You have done so many things. You have created everything so wisely. The earth is full of Your riches, and Your beautiful creations. The wonders You have done – all the miracles and great acts – are too numerous to count. No one can compare with You!

When You created the world, you looked upon all You had made, and indeed, it was very good. I agree with You, Father, all You have made is good! I declare, with utmost thanksgiving, that every good thing given, and every perfect gift is from above, coming from You, Wondrous Father. You are the Creator and

Sustainer of the Heavens; You created the sun, moon and stars; You are the Amazing Father of Lights!

While these lights were created, You are uncreated and eternal. The sun may rise and set, and its light may change and turn. But Your light never shifts or fades. You are perfect, and You never change. You are always the Light of the world, from everlasting to everlasting! Father, I trust in Your goodness, grace, wisdom, and Your consistency of character.

I trust Your wisdom, that You knew what You were doing as You created the world, and when You created us anew through Christ Jesus. Since everything You have created is good, I do not reject any of it, but I receive it with thanksgiving. That includes all the gifts and blessings You have given to me. It also includes the unique giftings, gracious divine endowments, talents and qualities You have given me; to give to others and put Your artistry on display!

Yes, Father, I even thank You for the gift of myself! You crafted me as a gift, and gave me to the world! Oh Father, what an amazing realization. Your scripture says everything You created is very good, and not to be rejected, but received with thanksgiving. So, with full acceptance, I thank You for me. I am Your good creation. I am a gift from above, coming down from the Father of Lights!

Thank You for the amazing way You created me! You've made me so wonderfully complex and marvelous. How intricately and how carefully I have been crafted in the hands of my Heavenly Father. I was made in the very image and likeness of God. I will give all my praise and thanks to You, because I am awesomely, remarkably, fearfully, and wonderfully made. Your workmanship is marvelous, and wonderful are Your works: my soul knows it very well.

In truth, every precious being You have created is wonderfully made. Cause me to see myself, and others, the way that You see us: with the heart of the Creator, the Redeemer, and the Father. How beautifully diverse Your creation is; how manifold are Your miraculous works! You made them all so wisely. Lord God, many are the wonders You have done, and the things You planned for us. If I tried to tell them all, there would be too many to count.

Father I ask You to reveal the plans You have had for me. Show me what You created me for, and redeemed me for. Purify my thoughts and desires, to line up with Your original plans for me, as You give me the grace to will and work for Your good pleasure. I want to live the glorious life You created me for!

Every good action, or act of giving is also from You. You know the works You have set out for us to do, and given us grace for. Your grace is manifold, many sided, unmeasured and overflowing. You were so immeasurably kind, that not only did You redeem us through Christ Jesus, You have also empowered us supernaturally to live out Your Heavenly purposes.

And You have given each believer unique parts of Your manifold grace. By Your grace, You have poured out extremely diverse powers and particular gifts, gracious divine endowments, spiritual talents, faculties, and qualities; upon different people, for different times and occasions, according to Your wisdom.

Heavenly Father, I yearn to take hold of these gifts! Open my eyes, by the Holy Spirit, to what You have given me, and want to give through me. And I pray that You would fill me with a passion to steward these gifts well, as a good trustee of Your grace, by employing these gifts to minister to my brothers and sisters in Christ, and to the world around me. I want to be a true servant of Your unmeasured grace, and freely give out what I've freely received.

Father, I thank You for the diversity of graces You give, that Jesus gives, and the Spirit gives. I praise You for the miraculous spiritual gifts that You give through the church! And though there may be many kinds of gifts, I acknowledge it is the same Spirit who gives them. Holy Spirit, manifest powerfully through me, and through others in my community, so that we can help each other, and for the profit of all!

Give us the desire to steward the gifts well, by using them to serve each other, and remove any comparison or competition from our minds. Help us see that we are one in Christ. We are His body, each a different member with our own gifts. And like the human body – with its many parts, all members of one another – there is no one part that is not important. There is no competition, for we are all edified when someone shares their gift faithfully. Father I ask that You cause a great gratitude for each other to stir within us. Help me, and help all of us, to see as You see!

We are the body of Christ, who is the head of the body, His church. Father, thank You for giving us unity and direction, and empowering us by the Holy Spirit. I ask that Your grace would continue to shine bright and manifest in my life, that I may do my part. Thank You for all You have done! In Christ's Holy name, I pray, Amen!

19

ABUNDANT GRACE: MORE THAN ENOUGH FOR EVERYTHING

2 Corinthians 9:8, Ephesians 3:20, Philippians 4:19, 1 Timothy 6:17, 1 John 4:16, John 3:16, Romans 8:32, Luke 12:32

2 Corinthians 9:8

And God is able to make all grace abound toward you, that you, always having all sufficiency in all things, may have an abundance for every good work. *(NKJV)*

And God is able to make every grace overflow to you, so that in every way, always having everything you need, you may excel in every good work. *(HCSB)*

And God is able to give you all grace in full measure; so that ever having enough of all things, you may be full of every good work. *(BBE)*

And God is able to make all grace [every favor and earthly blessing] come in abundance to you, so that you may always [under all circumstances, regardless of the need] have complete sufficiency in everything [being completely self-sufficient in Him], and have an abundance for every good work and act of charity. *(AMP)*

Ephesians 3:20

Now all glory to God, who is able, through his mighty power at work within us, to accomplish infinitely more than we might ask or think. *(NLT)*

Now to Him Who, by (in consequence of) the [action of His] power that is at work within us, is able to [carry out His purpose and] do superabundantly, far over and above all that we [dare] ask or think [infinitely beyond our highest prayers, desires, thoughts, hopes, or dreams] *(AMPC)*

Philippians 4:19

And my God shall supply all your need according to his riches in glory by Christ Jesus. *(NKJV)*

... My God will meet [supply; fulfill] all of your needs from [according to] his wonderful riches [glorious riches; or riches in heaven/glory] in Christ Jesus. *(EXB)*

1 Timothy 6:17

Command those who are rich in this present age not to be haughty, nor to trust in uncertain riches but in the living God, who gives us richly all things to enjoy. *(NKJV)*

As for the rich in this world, charge them not to be proud and arrogant and contemptuous of others, nor to set their hopes on uncertain riches, but on God, Who richly and ceaselessly provides us with everything for [our] enjoyment. *(AMPC)*

1 John 4:16

And we have known and believed the love that God has for us. God is love, and he who abides in love abides in God, and God in him. *(NKJV)*

And we know (understand, recognize, are conscious of, by observation and by experience) and believe (adhere to and put faith in and rely on) the love God cherishes for us. God is love, and he who dwells and continues in love dwells and continues in God, and God dwells and continues in him. *(AMPC)*

We know how much God loves us, and we have put our trust in his love. God is love, and all who live in love live in God, and God lives in them. *(NLT)*

... God is love, and the one who remains in love remains in God ... *(NASB)*

John 3:16

For God so loved the world that he gave his one and only Son, that whoever believes in him shall not perish but have eternal life. *(NIV)*

For God so greatly loved and dearly prized the world that He [even] gave up His only begotten (unique) Son, so that whoever believes in (trusts in, clings to, relies on) Him shall not perish (come to destruction, be lost) but have eternal (everlasting) life. *(AMPC)*

Romans 8:32

He who did not spare his own Son but gave him up for us all, how will he not also with him graciously give us all things? *(ESV)*

He who did not withhold or spare [even] His own Son but gave Him up for us all, will He not also with Him freely and graciously give us all [other] things? *(AMPC)*

Luke 12:32

Fear not, little flock; for it is your Father's good pleasure to give you the kingdom. *(KJV)*

So don't be afraid, little flock. For it gives your Father great happiness to give you the Kingdom. *(NLT)*
... your Father delights in giving you the kingdom. *(CEB)*

PRAYING THE WORD OF GRACE

Gracious Heavenly Father, You are the giver of all good things! Your very nature is giving: it's who You are, and it's what You do. You give because You love, and Your love is perfect. Your love never fails.

Father, I thank You for Your everlasting love. I have observed and experienced the love You have for me. Oh how deeply You cherish me! So I put my trust in You, and in Your love. Father, I pray that You would reveal the magnitude of Your love for me, that dwells within me. I pray that I would understand, recognize, become conscious of, and intimately know through experience, the love that You have for me. By Your grace and Holy Spirit, I pray I would abide and rest in Your love.

Not only do You have love for me, You are love itself. As I dwell and continue in love, I dwell and continue in God, and God dwells and continues in me. I live in love. I remain in love. I ask that You move me to believe in, trust in, adhere to, and rely on Your love, even more than I ever have before! Empower me to live in Your love, and remain in Your love, in much deeper ways. You are love, and Your love is infinite toward us! And because You love, You give.

In fact, You greatly loved and dearly prized the world so much, that You even gave Your one and only Son to us! You gave Him so that whoever believes and trusts in Him, will not perish but have eternal life. You gave Your Son so I would not come to destruction or be lost. Jesus, I am found in You. I cling to You, and I lean on You. Thank You, Father, for the eternal life You have given me in Jesus!

And if You did not spare Your own Son, but gave Him up for us all; how would You not also, with Him, graciously give us all things? Oh Father, I thank You that You didn't withhold Your very best, Your very own Son! So just as I trusted in Your greatest gift, I will also trust in Your giving heart: that You will also, with Jesus, freely and graciously give all other things!

I do not trust in the uncertain riches of this world: but I trust in You, the living God! Father, keep me from pride, arrogance and contempt of others. Keep my hope from uncertain riches. Transform my heart to be fully reliant on You, for You give us richly all things to enjoy. Father I thank You, that You richly and ceaselessly provide me with everything for my enjoyment. Your grace is inexhaustible! Your favor is immeasurable!

I will not be afraid, for Jesus is my Good Shepherd and takes good care of me. And You are My Father, and it is Your good pleasure to give me the Kingdom. It is Your great happiness to give to me. Yes, You delight in giving me the Kingdom!

Father, I thank You that You will supply and fulfill all my need, according to Your wonderful, glorious riches in Heaven in Christ Jesus. I thank You, and give all glory to You! You are able, through Your mighty power at work within me, to accomplish infinitely more than I might ask or think. Yes, You are able, by the action and power of the Holy Spirit within me, to carry out Your purpose, and do superabundantly, far over and above all that I dare ask or think: infinitely beyond my highest prayers, desires, thoughts, hopes or dreams. Wow! I have not yet even imagined what You can do, and the glorious things You want to do! How wonderful Your thoughts must be!

And You are able, God, to give me all grace in full measure. You make every grace – every favor, empowerment, and earthly blessing – come in abundance and overflow to me. You do this so that in every way – under all circumstances and regardless of the need – I have complete sufficiency in everything, and have an abundance for every good work and act of love. I always have all sufficiency in all things, and I am completely self-sufficient in Christ's sufficiency. I always have enough of all things, so I may excel in every good work. I am completely full!

Father, thank You for always giving me everything I need, according to Your riches in glory in Christ, and giving me richly all things to enjoy. Thank You for doing and giving far beyond where my imagination can go. I ask that You give me a brave, childlike heart to fully trust Your love, to seek You for grace in abundance, and to pray big prayers, according to Your glorious riches in Christ. I ask all these things in His wonderful name, Amen!

20

REIGNING IN LIFE: GRACE OVERFLOWS AND OVERCOMES

Romans 5:17, Romans 5:20-21, Romans 8:31, Zechariah 4:7, 1 Corinthians 3:16, Romans 8:37, John 19:30, Revelation 21:6-7

Romans 5:17

For if by the one man's offense death reigned through the one, much more those who receive abundance of grace and of the gift of righteousness will reign in life through the One, Jesus Christ. *(NKJV)*

For the sin of this one man, Adam, caused death to rule over many. But even greater is God's wonderful grace and his gift of righteousness, for all who receive it will live in triumph over sin and death through this one man, Jesus Christ. *(NLT)*

... much more surely will those who receive [God's] overflowing grace (unmerited favor) and the free gift of righteousness [putting them into right standing with Himself] reign as kings in life through the one Man Jesus Christ (the Messiah, the Anointed One). *(AMPC)*

Romans 5:20-21

Now the law came in to increase the trespass, but where sin increased, grace abounded all the more, so that, as sin reigned in death, grace also might reign through righteousness leading to eternal life through Jesus Christ our Lord. *(ESV)*

... But as people sinned more and more, God's wonderful grace became more abundant ... *(NLT)* ... but where sin abounded grace has overabounded. *(DARBY)* ... but where sin increased, grace multiplied even more ... *(CEB)* ... but where there was much sin, there was much more grace ... *(BBE)*

... But where sin increased, [God's remarkable, gracious gift of] grace [His unmerited favor] has surpassed it and increased all the more, so that, as sin reigned in death, so also grace would reign through righteousness which brings eternal life through Jesus Christ our Lord. *(AMP)*

... So just as sin ruled over all people and brought them to death, now God's wonderful grace rules instead ... *(NLT)*

Romans 8:31

What then shall we say to these things? If God is for us, who can be against us? *(NKJV)*

Zechariah 4:7

What are you, O great mountain [of obstacles]? Before Zerubbabel [who will rebuild the temple] you will become a plain (insignificant)! And he will bring out the capstone [of the new temple] with loud shouts of "Grace, grace to it!" *(AMP)*

1 Corinthians 3:16

Do you not know that you are the temple of God and that the Spirit of God dwells in you? *(NKJV)*

Romans 8:37

No, despite all these things, overwhelming victory is ours through Christ, who loved us. *(NLT)*

But in all these things we overcome, because of him that hath loved us. *(DRA)*

But in all these things we are completely victorious through God [or Christ; the One] who showed his love for us. *(EXB)*

John 19:30

When he had received the drink, Jesus said, "It is finished." ... *(NIV)* ... "[completed; accomplished]." ... *(EXB)* ... All is done. And with his head bent he gave up his spirit. *(BBE)*

Revelation 21:6-7

And he also said, "It is finished! I am the Alpha and the Omega—the Beginning and the End. To all who are thirsty I will give freely from the springs of the water of life. All who are victorious will inherit all these blessings, and I will be their God, and they will be my children" *(NLT)*

... He who overcomes shall inherit all things, and I will be his God and he shall be My son ... *(NKJV)*

PRAYING THE WORD OF GRACE

Almighty Father, and Victorious Lord and Savior, Jesus Christ: You have won! Grace overflows and overcomes through Christ and His finished work! Hallelujah!

By the sin of one man, Adam, death reigned through that one. But God, You are so good, and have defeated death through the One, Jesus Christ! Your wonderful grace and Your free gift of righteousness were, and are, and will always be: far greater than sin or death in every way!

Father, I thank You for Your abundant, conquering grace. Sin may have increased over time, and did so through the law. But wherever sin increased, grace has surpassed it, and increased all the more. As people sinned more and more, Your wonderful grace became more abundant. Where sin abounded, Your remarkable gift of amazing grace has abounded all the more. Yes, grace overabounded and multiplied! I overflow with gratitude and joy, as I behold the glorious overflow of grace: that wherever there was much sin, there was so much more grace!

So if by the one man's offense, death reigned through the one: how much more surely will those who receive Your overflowing grace and the free gift of righteousness reign in life through the One, Jesus Christ? Yes, Father, I agree with Your word and receive the truth, along with Your free gift. As I freely receive Your grace, unmerited favor and righteousness through Christ, I will live in triumph over sin and death, through Him. I receive the overflow of Your grace! I am freely in right standing with You, Father, by Your amazing gift! All who simply receive Your gifts will reign as kings and queens in life. Thank You, Gracious Father!

How remarkable this is! Sin used to rule over all and bring us to death. Now Your wonderful grace rules instead. Grace reigns through righteousness which brings eternal life through Jesus Christ our Lord. I receive the abundance of grace, and the free gift of righteousness, and eternal life through Christ Jesus: and I reign in life!

And God, if You are for me, who can be against me? Nothing can stand against You, Almighty God! Just as Zerubbabel rebuilt the temple of God in times of old, You have rebuilt me as Your temple now, and the Spirit of God dwells within me. I ask that You cause me to know the gravity and power of this revelation.

Zechariah spoke boldly to the mountain of obstacles they faced. And just as he spoke, so do I: What mountain can stand before the mighty temple of God, overflowing with grace and the Holy Spirit? Before You, Your grace, and Your temple: every mountain is an insignificant plain! As I see what You have done in me, and gaze with wonder at the glory of Christ Jesus, I shout ecstatically with all God's people, "Grace! Grace!"

Truly, in all things I am completely victorious through Christ, the one who showed Your love for us. Because of You and Your amazing love – though I may face trials and tribulation – despite all these things, overwhelming victory is mine through Christ. In all things I overcome, because of You, Father!

You finished the work at the Cross of Jesus Christ. You overcame the power of sin and death, and overcame darkness with light. It is finished. It is completed. It is accomplished. And You freely give the victory to all who receive Your Son. And I receive Him with open arms!

You are the Alpha and the Omega, the Beginning and the End! You give freely from the springs of the water of life to all who are thirsty. I freely drink from Your river of life! I have Your victory in Christ, and overcome in all things! I inherit all things, and all blessings, and You are my God, and I am Your child!

Father, I ask that You open the eyes of my heart to Your glorious victory in Christ. Reveal to me the all-sufficient and surpassing riches of Your grace, and the holiness and strength of the temple You made me to be. Teach me to speak grace over every obstacle, and show me how to reign in life through the over-flow of grace and the gift of righteousness. Lead me in the way of Your eternal life through Christ Jesus, our Lord. In His name I pray, Amen!

21

CHRIST'S UNSHAKABLE VICTORY AND AWESOME GIFT

Romans 6:23, 2 Corinthians 9:15, Psalm 63:3,
1 Corinthians 15:57, 2 Corinthians 2:14, Colossians 2:15,
Hebrews 2:14, Hebrews 12:28

Romans 6:23

For the wages of sin is death, but the free gift of God [that is, His remarkable, overwhelming gift of grace to believers] is eternal life in Christ Jesus our Lord. *(AMP)*

2 Corinthians 9:15

Thanks be to God for His indescribable gift! *(NKJV)*

Now thanks be to God for His Gift, [precious] beyond telling [His indescribable, inexpressible, free Gift]! *(AMPC)*

Thank God for this gift too wonderful for words! *(NLT)* ... [which is precious beyond words]! *(AMP)*

Psalm 63:3

Because Your lovingkindness is better than life, my lips shall praise You. *(NKJV)*

My lips will glorify You because Your faithful love is better than life. *(HCSB)*

... Your favor ... *(NASB)* ... your mercy ... *(BBE)* ... Your unfailing love is better than life itself; how I praise you! *(NLT)*

1 Corinthians 15:57

But thanks be to God, who gives us the victory through our Lord Jesus Christ! *(HCSB)*

But praise be to God who gives us strength to overcome through our Lord Jesus Christ. *(BBE)*

2 Corinthians 2:14

Now thanks be to God, who always leads us in triumph in Christ, and reveals through us the sweet aroma of his knowledge in every place. *(WEB)*

But thanks be to God, Who in Christ always leads us in triumph [as trophies of Christ's victory] ... *(AMPC)* ... and continues to lead us along in Christ's triumphal procession. Now he uses us to spread the knowledge of Christ everywhere, like a sweet perfume ... *(NLT)* ... and through us diffuses the fragrance of His knowledge ... *(NKJV)* ... and the fragrance of His knowledge He is manifesting through us in every place. *(YLT)*

Colossians 2:15

And having disarmed the powers and authorities, he made a public spectacle of them, triumphing over them by the cross. *(NIV)*

When He had disarmed the rulers and authorities [those supernatural forces of evil operating against us], He made a public example of them [exhibiting them as captives in His triumphal procession], having triumphed over them through the cross. *(AMP)*

God [or Christ; He] stripped the spiritual rulers and powers of their authority [disarmed/despoiled the rulers and authorities]. With the cross, he won the victory and showed the world that they were powerless [publicly shamed them; made a public spectacle of them; like a triumphant general displaying his captives in a victory parade]. *(EXB)*

Hebrews 2:14

Therefore, since the children share in flesh and blood, He Himself likewise also partook of the same, so that through death He might destroy the one who has the power of death, that is, the devil, and free those who through fear of death were subject to slavery all their lives. *(NASB)*

Therefore, since [these His] children share in flesh and blood [the physical nature of mankind], He Himself in a similar manner also shared in the same [physical nature, but without sin], so that through [experiencing] death He might make powerless (ineffective, impotent) him who had the power of death—that is, the devil— and [that He] might free all those who through [the haunting] fear of death were held in slavery throughout their lives. *(AMP)*

Because God's children are human beings—made of flesh and blood—the Son also became flesh and blood. For only as a human being could he die, and only by dying could he break the power of the devil, who had the power of death. Only in this way could he set free all who have lived their lives as slaves to the fear of dying. *(NLT)*

Hebrews 12:28

Therefore let us be grateful for receiving a kingdom that cannot be shaken, and thus let us offer to God acceptable worship, with reverence and awe. *(ESV)*

Praying the Word of Grace

Awesome Heavenly Father, and Wonderful Jesus: King of Kings, and Lord of Lords! I thank You, God, for Your indescribable gift! It is precious beyond telling, too wonderful for words! Thank You for the inexpressible free gift of everlasting life!

Yes, the wages of sin is death. But Your remarkable, overwhelming gift of grace is eternal life in Christ Jesus our Lord. You gave us this gift because of Your unconditional, amazing love with which You loved us.

Oh Father, my lips will glorify You and praise You, because Your faithful love is better than life! Yes, Your unfailing loving-kindness, Your unmerited favor, Your unending mercy, and Your unlimited grace: they are better than life itself!

I thank You, Father, that You give me the victory through our Lord Jesus Christ. You give me strength to overcome by Your grace through Him.

The eternal victory is Yours forever and ever! You have defeated sin and death, and all our enemies. You disarmed the powers, rulers and authorities, those supernatural forces of evil operating against us. Then You made a public spectacle of them, like a triumphant general displaying his captives in a victory parade. You triumphed over all these evil forces in the Cross of Christ. You won the victory, stripped the spiritual rulers and powers of authority, and showed the world that these forces were powerless. I praise You, Victorious God!

Jesus, You became flesh and blood, just like us, and shared in our humanity. You died on the Cross, taking our own sin and death with You. Through Your death and resurrection, You destroyed the one who had the power of death. You destroyed the devil and broke his power! You made him powerless, ineffective and impotent. And in doing so, You freed all those who were held in slavery their whole lives by the haunting fear of death. Through Your free gift of eternal life, You have set me free from the fear of death. Wow!

And I thank You, Father God, that I am Your prize! You lead me in Your triumphal procession, as a trophy of Christ's victory. You diffuse through me the sweet aroma of the knowledge of Christ everywhere. You manifest Your victory, salvation and grace through me. I have been set free for all time! I ask that You would reveal Yourself to me – and through me – more and more.

I praise You, God, for Your overwhelming grace upon grace, and the victory which You have given me in Christ, having delivered me from my enemies and the power of death. I praise You! Since I am receiving a kingdom that cannot be shaken, I am forever humbled and utterly grateful, God. May the worship I offer You be an acceptable response to this magnificent truth.

I ask that You reveal in greater measure the power and wonder of Christ's unshakable victory and awesome gift, so that I may be overwhelmed with greater reverence and awe for You, worship You all the more, and diffuse the fragrance of Your knowledge in every place I go! In Christ's Majestic name I pray, Amen!

22

UNLIMITED ACCESS TO ALL THE PROMISES OF GOD

Ephesians 1:3, 2 Peter 1:2-4, Romans 5:2, Ephesians 3:12, 2 Corinthians 1:20, Philemon 1:6

Ephesians 1:3

Blessed be the God and Father of our Lord Jesus Christ, who has blessed us with every spiritual blessing in the heavenly places in Christ *(NKJV)*

All praise to God, the Father of our Lord Jesus Christ, who has blessed us with every spiritual blessing in the heavenly realms because we are united with Christ. *(NLT)*

2 Peter 1:2-4

May grace and peace be multiplied to you through the knowledge of God and of Jesus our Lord. His divine power has given us everything required for life and godliness through the knowledge of Him who called us by His own glory and goodness. By these He has given us very great and precious promises, so that through them you may share in the divine nature, escaping the corruption that is in the world because of evil desires. *(HCSB)*

May grace (God's favor) and peace (which is perfect well-being, all necessary good, all spiritual prosperity, and freedom from fears and agitating passions and moral conflicts) be multiplied to you in [the full, personal, precise, and correct] knowledge of God and of Jesus our Lord.

For His divine power has bestowed upon us all things that [are requisite and suited] to life and godliness, through the [full, personal] knowledge of Him Who called us by and to His own glory and excellence (virtue).

By means of these He has bestowed on us His precious and exceedingly great promises, so that through them you may escape [by flight] from the moral decay (rottenness and corruption) that is in the world because of covetousness (lust and greed), and become sharers (partakers) of the divine nature. *(AMPC)*

... And because of his glory and excellence, he has given us great and precious promises ... *(NLT)* ... For by these He has bestowed on us His precious and magnificent promises [of inexpressible value] ... *(AMP)*

Romans 5:2

We have also obtained access through Him by faith into this grace in which we stand, and we rejoice in the hope of the glory of God. *(HCSB)*

Because of our faith, Christ has brought us into this place of undeserved privilege where we now stand, and we confidently and joyfully look forward to sharing God's glory. *(NLT)*

Through Him we also have access by faith into this [remarkable state of] grace in which we [firmly and safely and securely] stand. Let us rejoice in our hope and the confident assurance of [experiencing and enjoying] the glory of [our great] God [the manifestation of His excellence and power]. *(AMP)*

Ephesians 3:12

In Him we have boldness and confident access through faith in Him. *(HCSB)*

... We can do this through faith in Christ [or because of Christ's faithfulness]. *(EXB)*

2 Corinthians 1:20

For no matter how many promises God has made, they are "Yes" in Christ. And so through him the "Amen" is spoken by us to the glory of God. *(NIV)*

For all of God's promises have been fulfilled in Christ with a resounding "Yes!" And through Christ, our "Amen" (which means "Yes") ascends to God for his glory. *(NLT)*

Philemon 1:6

... that the sharing of your faith may become effective by the acknowledgment of every good thing which is in you in Christ Jesus. *(NKJV)*

[And I pray] that the participation in and sharing of your faith may produce and promote full recognition and appreciation and understanding and precise knowledge of every good [thing] that is ours in [our identification with] Christ Jesus [and unto His glory]. *(AMPC)*

And I am praying that you will put into action the generosity that comes from your faith as you understand and experience all the good things we have in Christ. *(NLT)*

I pray that the faith you share [the sharing/fellowship of your faith] may make you [enable/empower you to] understand every blessing we have in Christ. *(EXB)*

Praying the Word of Grace

Blessed Heavenly Father, I thank You for Your limitless goodness and grace! I pour out all my worship to You! You have blessed me with every spiritual blessing in the heavenly realms because I am united with Christ. Your grace and peace are multiplied to me as I increase in knowledge of You and of Jesus Your Son. I am filled to overflowing with Your very life!

Father, I ask You – according to Your abundant grace, by the power of Your Spirit dwelling within me – that I would powerfully encounter You, and know You fully. I long to know You by experience, with increasing amounts of full, personal, precise and correct knowledge. As I experience intimately knowing You more and more, Your grace and peace overflow within me, throughout all my being.

Father, thank You for Your peace that You give me, which is perfect well-being, all necessary good, all spiritual prosperity, and freedom from fears and agitating passions and moral conflicts. What a precious gift!

Thank You, Father, that Your divine power has given me everything required for life and godliness. I can access all of it through the knowledge of You and Your Son. I thank You for Your goodness, Your glory, Your excellence and virtue. It is by these, and unto these, which You have called me. Because of these, and by means of these, You have also bestowed upon me Your precious and magnificent promises, of inexpressible value.

Through Your very great and precious promises, I share in Your divine nature! I have escaped the corruption that is in the world because of lust, greed, and evil desires.

Father, I thank You for this remarkable state of grace in which I stand: this place of undeserved privilege; and the very divine nature, presence and shared life of Christ! I firmly, safely, and securely stand in Your wonderful grace. And through Christ, by believing in Him: I have full access to all of this grace, and all of Your promises. This is amazing beyond words!

I confidently and joyfully look forward to sharing God's glory! Yes, I rejoice in this hope! Through Christ, I have the confident assurance of experiencing and enjoying the glory of our great God. I get to experience and enjoy the manifestation of Your excellence and power, and all because of Christ's faithfulness. Oh, how great is Your faithfulness!

In Christ, I have boldness and confident access, through faith in Him. For no matter how many promises You have made, they are "Yes" in Christ. Truly, I believe that all of Your promises have been fulfilled in Him with a resounding, "Yes!" And so, through Christ, I respond with my exuberant "Yes" and "Amen!" You are glorified by my radical acceptance of Your radical gift! May my "yes" through Christ ascend to You for Your glory!

I pray that the faith You've given me in Christ may produce in me a full recognition, appreciation, understanding, and precise knowledge of every good thing that is mine in Christ. As I participate and share in Your faith, and identify with Christ Himself, I thank You that this faith enables and empowers me to understand and experience every blessing I have in Him. May I have the full revelation by Your Spirit to acknowledge every good thing which is in me. As I come to know by faith, all that I have by grace, a generosity wells up inside of me, along with a desire to freely give what I've freely received. This overflow of grace is all to Your glory!

May I take hold of all of that for which Christ Jesus took hold of me. I open my arms wide to receive all of Your magnificent and precious promises, which are all fulfilled in Christ. I agree with You, and receive the truth, that they are all "Yes" in Him. You have lavished them on me already! I pray that You would open my heart to become more aware of You, to know You more, and to understand what I already have and who I already am in Christ. And help me to access all of these promises with bold and confident faith, through Christ. It is in His immeasurably powerful name I pray, Amen!

23

SHARING IN THE DIVINE NATURE

1 Timothy 1:14, 2 Peter 1:4, 1 Peter 1:23, Colossians 1:6,
Galatians 5:22-23, 2 Corinthians 3:17-18, Ephesians 4:23-24

1 Timothy 1:14

The grace of our Lord was poured out on me abundantly, along with the faith and love that are in Christ Jesus. *(NIV)*

Oh, how generous and gracious our Lord was! He filled me with the faith and love that come from Christ Jesus. *(NLT)*

And the grace (unmerited favor and blessing) of our Lord [actually] flowed out superabundantly and beyond measure for me ... *(AMPC)*

But the grace of our Lord was fully given [overflowed; abounded] to me, and with that grace came the faith and love that are in Christ Jesus. *(EXB)*

2 Peter 1:4

Through these He has granted to us His precious and magnificent promises, so that by them you may become partakers of the divine nature, having escaped the corruption that is in the world on account of lust. *(NASB)*

And because of his glory and excellence, he has given us great and precious promises. These are the promises that enable you to share his divine nature and escape the world's corruption caused by human desires. *(NLT)*

1 Peter 1:23

For you have been born again [that is, reborn from above—spiritually transformed, renewed, and set apart for His purpose] not of seed which is perishable but [from that which is] imperishable and immortal, that is, through the living and everlasting word of God. *(AMP)*

Colossians 1:6

This same Good News that came to you is going out all over the world. It is bearing fruit everywhere by changing lives, just as it changed your lives from the day you first heard and understood the truth about God's wonderful grace. *(NLT)*

... Indeed, in the whole world [that Gospel] is bearing fruit and still is growing [by its own inherent power], even as it has done among yourselves ever since the day you first heard and came to know and understand the grace of God in truth. [You came to know the grace or undeserved favor of God in reality, deeply and clearly and thoroughly, becoming accurately and intimately acquainted with it.] *(AMPC)*

Galatians 5:22-23

But the fruit of the Spirit is love, joy, peace, patience, kindness, goodness, faithfulness, gentleness, and self-control ... *(CSB)*

But the Holy Spirit produces this kind of fruit in our lives ... *(NLT)* But the fruit of the Spirit [the result of His presence within us] ... *(AMP)* ... [the work which His presence within accomplishes] is love, joy (gladness), peace, patience (an even temper, forbearance), kindness, goodness (benevolence), faithfulness, gentleness (meekness, humility), self-control (self-restraint) ... *(AMPC)*

2 Corinthians 3:17-18

Now the Lord is the Spirit, and where the Spirit of the Lord is, there is freedom. We all, with unveiled faces, are looking as in a mirror at the glory of the Lord and are being transformed into the same image from glory to glory; this is from the Lord who is the Spirit. *(HCSB)*

Ephesians 4:23-24

You are being renewed in the spirit of your minds; you put on the new self, the one created according to God's likeness in righteousness and purity of the truth. *(HCSB)*

Instead, let the Spirit renew your thoughts and attitudes. Put on your new nature, created to be like God—truly righteous and holy. *(NLT)*

... and be continually renewed in the spirit of your mind [having a fresh, untarnished mental and spiritual attitude], and put on the new self [the regenerated and renewed nature], created in God's image, [godlike] in the righteousness and holiness of the truth [living in a way that expresses to God your gratitude for your salvation]. *(AMP)*

Praying the Word of Grace

Generous Heavenly Father, Gracious Lord Jesus, Glorious Holy Spirit: Thank You, for You have fully given Your grace, unmerited favor and blessing to me. The grace of Jesus Christ has been poured out on me abundantly! Your grace has truly and actually overflowed for me, far beyond measure. And with that grace, You filled me with the faith and love that are in Christ Jesus.

Because of Your glory and excellence, and through Your goodness and grace, You have given me Your precious and magnificent promises. These are the promises that enable me to share Your divine nature. Yes! I have become a partaker of the divine nature of God, and I have escaped the corruption that is in the world on account of lust.

For I have been born again in Christ. I have been spiritually transformed, renewed, and set apart for Your purpose, Father. Reborn from above, not of seed which is perishable, but from that which is imperishable and immortal. I have been born again through the living and everlasting Word of God!

This word of grace – the same Good News that came to me – is going out all over the world. Bearing fruit everywhere and still growing by its own inherent power. The word of grace is changing lives, just as it changed my life from the day I first heard and understood the truth about God's wonderful grace.

Father, I pray that I come to know Your grace in reality – deeply, clearly and thoroughly, becoming accurately and intimately acquainted with it – so that it would produce more and more fruit within me, by Your Holy Spirit.

Holy Spirit, I thank You that You continually produce amazing fruit in my life, which is the result of Your presence with me. Within me, the Holy Spirit produces love, joy, peace, patience, kindness, goodness, faithfulness, gentleness, and self-control. This is who I am, by the power of Your grace and Spirit!

Holy Spirit, You are Lord! You are within me; and wherever You are, there is freedom! There is true liberty on the inside of me. I behold the glory of the Lord with an unveiled face, and as I behold You, it's as if I'm looking in a mirror. By Your power and grace, I am transformed into Your same image, from glory to glory. I behold You with wide-eyed wonder! I am transformed and I am free!

I thank You that I am being continually renewed in the spirit of my mind. By the Spirit of God, I am taking on a fresh, untarnished mental and spiritual attitude. Holy Spirit, I allow You to renew my thoughts and attitudes. I have put on my new self, my new nature, which is created in God's image, to be like God. I thank You, Father, for my regenerated and renewed nature I have in Christ, which is like You, truly righteous and holy, in the purity of the truth. You have empowered me and enabled me by Your grace to be like You. May I live in such a way that expresses to You my gratitude for my salvation.

Father, I ask that You continue to renew my mind, by the power of the Holy Spirit, so that I may fully know and experience this glorious new nature You have given me in Christ, by Your grace. It is in His name that I pray, Amen!

THE GLORIOUS MYSTERY OF GRACE
REVEALED IN CHRIST

*2 Timothy 1:9-10, Titus 1:2, Ephesians 3:11, Colossians 1:27,
John 1:18, Hebrews 1:3, Colossians 1:15, 1 John 1:1-5*

2 Timothy 1:9-10

[God] hath saved us, and called us with an holy calling, not according to our works, but according to his own purpose and grace, which was given us in Christ Jesus before the world began,

But is now made manifest by the appearing of our Saviour Jesus Christ, who hath abolished death, and hath brought life and immortality to light through the gospel *(KJV)*

... He did this, not because we deserved it, but because that was his plan from before the beginning of time—to show us his grace through Christ Jesus. And now he has made all of this plain to us by the appearing of Christ Jesus, our Savior. He broke the power of death and illuminated the way to life and immortality through the Good News. *(NLT)*

... because of His own purpose and grace [His amazing, undeserved favor] which was granted to us in Christ Jesus before the world began [eternal ages ago], but now [that extraordinary purpose and grace] has been fully disclosed and realized by us through the appearing of our Savior Christ Jesus who [through His incarnation and earthly ministry] abolished death [making it null and void] and brought life and immortality to light through the gospel. *(AMP)*

Titus 1:2

This truth gives them confidence that they have eternal life, which God—who does not lie—promised them before the world began. *(NLT)*

[Resting] in the hope of eternal life, [life] which the ever truthful God Who cannot deceive promised before the world or the ages of time began. *(AMPC)*

Ephesians 3:11

This is according to His eternal purpose accomplished in Christ Jesus our Lord. *(HCSB)*

This was his eternal plan, which he carried out through Christ Jesus our Lord. *(NLT)*

Colossians 1:27

... to whom God would make known what are the riches of the glory of this mystery among the nations, which is Christ in you the hope of glory *(DARBY)*

God decided [chose; willed] to let his people know this rich and glorious secret [mystery] which he has for all people [the nations/Gentiles]. This secret [mystery] is that Christ lives in you ... *(EXB)* ... which is Christ living in you, the hope of glory. *(CEB)*

John 1:18

No one has ever seen God. The one and only Son, who is himself God and is at the Father's side—he has revealed him. *(CSB)* ... The only begotten Son, who is in the bosom of the Father, He has declared Him. *(NKJV)*

No one has seen God [His essence, His divine nature] at any time; the [One and] only begotten God [that is, the unique Son] who is in the intimate presence of the Father, He has explained Him [and interpreted and revealed the awesome wonder of the Father]. *(AMP)*

Hebrews 1:3

The Son radiates God's own glory and expresses the very character of God, and he sustains everything by the mighty power of his command. When he had cleansed us from our sins, he sat down in the place of honor at the right hand of the majestic God in heaven. *(NLT)*

The Son is the radiance of God's glory and the exact representation of his being, sustaining all things by his powerful word ... *(NIV)* ... being the brightness of His glory and the express image of His person ... *(NKJV)* ... the very image of his substance ... *(WEB)*

The Son reflects [or radiates; shines forth] the glory of God [John 1:14] and shows exactly what God is like [is the exact representation/imprint/stamp of his being/essence/nature] ... *(EXB)*

The Son is the radiance and only expression of the glory of [our awesome] God [reflecting God's Shekinah glory, the Light-being, the brilliant light of the divine], and the exact representation and perfect imprint of His [Father's] essence, and upholding and maintaining and propelling all things [the entire physical and spiritual universe] by His powerful word [carrying the universe along to its predetermined goal] ... *(AMP)*

Colossians 1:15

The Son is the image of the invisible God, the firstborn over all creation. *(NIV)*

Christ is the visible image of the invisible God. He existed before anything was created and is supreme over all creation *(NLT)*

He is the exact living image [the essential manifestation] of the unseen God [the visible representation of the invisible], the firstborn [the preeminent one, the sovereign, and the originator] of all creation. *(AMP)*

1 John 1:1-5

We proclaim to you the one who existed from the beginning, whom we have heard and seen. We saw him with our own eyes and touched him with our own hands. He is the Word of life. This one who is life itself was revealed to us, and we have seen him. And now we testify and proclaim to you that he is the one who is eternal life. He was with the Father, and then he was revealed to us. We proclaim to you what we ourselves have actually seen and heard so that you may have fellowship with us. And our fellowship is with the Father and with his Son, Jesus Christ. We are writing these things so that you may fully share our joy.

This is the message we heard from Jesus and now declare to you: God is light, and there is no darkness in him at all. *(NLT)*

PRAYING THE WORD OF GRACE

Glorious Heavenly Father, I am struck with awe and wonder over the magnificence, kindness, and wisdom of Your eternal plans, purposes, and promises. Father, throughout the ages, You have always had a good plan. Your plan was to give us hope, and to give us life. And in our Lord Christ Jesus, Your Son, You carried out and accomplished Your eternal plan! You have done it all!

You saved us and You called us with a holy calling – not because we did anything to deserve it – but according to Your own purpose and grace, and undeserved favor. You granted us these in Christ Jesus before the world began. What a captivating mystery to contemplate!

Father, Your extraordinary purpose and grace have now been fully disclosed and realized by us through the appearing of Jesus Christ, our Savior. Thank

You, Father, for Your purpose and grace; which were made manifest through Your Son's incarnation, earthly ministry, death and resurrection.

Thank You, Jesus! You abolished death; breaking its power and making it null and void! And You illuminated the way to life and immortality through the Good News! And hearing and knowing the truth of Your gospel gives me confidence that I indeed have this eternal life.

Father, I thank You that I can rest in this hope, which is secure. Thank You that You are ever truthful, and cannot deceive or lie. You promised us eternal life before the world and time itself began, and You delivered on Your promise.

Thank You, Father, for giving me eternal life through Jesus! I share in Your life forever!

In Christ, You chose to let Your people know Your rich and glorious secret which You have for all people. In Him, Your mystery was revealed at last. By Your grace, You have revealed: Christ living in me, the hope of glory! In Christ, through faith in Him, You have revealed the plan of eternal life, and the mystery of union with God! This is a wonder too beautiful for words, and I pray I can experience the truth of it more and more!

I thank You, Wonderful Father, that Jesus also revealed You. In Him, we have finally seen Your true glory. No one had ever seen God. Then, according to Your gracious will, Your one and only Son became flesh and dwelt among us. Jesus is Himself God, and is in Your intimate presence, and from Your very heart, Father. He explained You, He declared You, and He interpreted You. Thank You, Jesus, for revealing the awesome wonder of the Father to me!

Jesus, I praise You, for You are the radiance of God's own glory, the brilliant light of God! You shine forth the Father's being and essence. You are the exact representation of the Father's being; the only full expression of His character; the very image of His substance; the perfect imprint of His essence and nature. You alone show us exactly what our awesome God is like. Jesus, You are the essential manifestation of the unseen; and the visible image of the invisible God.

Jesus, You sustain all things by the mighty power of Your word. You have cleansed us from our sins. And You are seated in the place of honor at the right hand of the majestic Father in Heaven. You existed before anything was created, and are supreme over all creation. You are the preeminent one, the sovereign and the originator of all creation.

The one who is supreme over all creation; the one who existed from the beginning, who upholds the world with His powerful word; the very radiance of God's glory and manifestation of God's being; the one who is Life itself: this same One lives in me! And I live in You, Christ, and I am seated with You in Heavenly places! Through You, I share in Your divine nature, and in the very glory of God!

I take a moment to let this breathtaking reality set in.

Father, I am enraptured by the revelation of Your Son: who revealed You, and Your glorious mysteries of grace. Thank You that You revealed Yourself through Your Son. Thank You for Your plan, and for Your first messengers, who got to see Jesus with their own eyes, hear Him with their own ears, and touch Him with their own hands. Thank You for their testimony which they proclaimed, and we now have in Scripture.

Father, I listen with rapt attention to their testimony, so that I may fully share their joy; and so I may have full fellowship with all the saints, and with the Father, Son, and Holy Spirit. I receive the message they heard from Jesus and now is declared unto me. You are Light, Father, and there is no darkness in You at all! This is the exact representation of Your glory, and the truth of who You are!

Heavenly Father, I pray for You to fill and flood my heart with light, by the power of the Holy Spirit working within me. May I take hold of every promise You have fulfilled in Christ. May I be able to deeply comprehend, and confidently stand in the hope of eternal life and immortality brought to light by Jesus Christ.

I pray that I may come to know the riches of Your glorious mystery, of Christ in me, the hope of glory. I pray that through Christ, who is eternal life Himself, I may behold Your glory fully, and come to know You through experience. I ask to truly and intimately know the love of my Father, the grace of Jesus Christ, and the communion and fellowship of the Holy Spirit. In the name of Jesus, I pray, Amen!

GOD SPEAKS THE WONDERFUL WORD OF GRACE

Luke 4:22, John 6:63, Psalm 45:1-2, Jeremiah 15:16, Psalm 119:103, Psalm 119:140, Psalm 19:7, Psalm 119:105, Hebrews 4:12, Psalm 107:20

Luke 4:22

All the people spoke well of Jesus and were amazed at the words of grace [or gracious words] he spoke. They asked, "Isn't this Joseph's son?" *(EXB)*

All testified about him, and wondered at the gracious words which proceeded out of his mouth ... *(WEB)* ... and admiring the gracious words ... *(NASB)* ... so impressed were they by the gracious words flowing from his lips ... *(CEB)*

John 6:63

The Spirit is the One who gives life. The flesh doesn't help at all. The words that I have spoken to you are spirit and are life. *(HCSB)*

It is the Spirit Who gives life [He is the Life-giver]; the flesh conveys no benefit whatever [there is no profit in it]. The words (truths) that I have been speaking to you are spirit and life. *(AMPC)*

Psalm 45:1-2

Beautiful words fill my mind [My heart is stirred with a good word].
I am speaking of royal things [or address my work to the king]... *(EXB)*

Beautiful words stir my heart.
I will recite a lovely poem about the king,
for my tongue is like the pen of a skillful poet.
You are the most handsome of all.
Gracious words stream from your lips.
God himself has blessed you forever. *(NLT)*

My heart is flowing over with good things ... *(BBE)*
My heart overflows with a pleasing theme ... *(ESV)*
My heart is welling forth [with] a good matter ... *(DARBY)*
My heart is moved by a noble theme as I recite my verses to the king ... *(CSB)*
... I address my psalm to the King ... *(AMP)*

... You are fairer than the children of men;
graciousness is poured upon Your lips ... *(AMPC)*
... Thou hast been beautified above the sons of men,
Grace hath been poured into thy lips ... *(YLT)*
... grace flows from your lips ... *(CSB)*

... You are the most excellent of men
and your lips have been anointed with grace,
since God has blessed you forever. *(NIV)*

Jeremiah 15:16

When your words came, I ate them;
they were my joy and my heart's delight,
for I bear your name, Lord God Almighty. *(NIV)*

When I discovered your words, I devoured them... *(NLT)*
When your words turned up, I feasted on them... *(CEB)*
... and I listened carefully to [ate] them ... *(EXB)*

... and thy word was to me a joy and gladness of my heart ... *(DRA)*

But to me your word is a joy, making my heart glad; for I am named by your name, O Lord God of armies. *(BBE)*

Psalm 119:103

How sweet are Your words to my taste!
Yes, sweeter than honey to my mouth! *(NASB)*

How sweet are your promises to my taste,
more than honey to my mouth! *(WEB)*

Psalm 119:140

Your word is completely pure, and Your servant loves it. *(HCSB)*

Your promises have been thoroughly tested; that is why I love them so much. *(NLT)*

Psalm 19:7

The instruction of the LORD is perfect,
renewing one's life;
the testimony of the LORD is trustworthy,
making the inexperienced wise. *(HCSB)*

The instructions of the Lord are perfect,
reviving the soul ... *(NLT)* ... restoring and refreshing the soul ... *(AMP)*

Psalm 119:105

Your word is a lamp to my feet
And a light to my path. *(NKJV)*

Your word is a lamp before my feet
and a light for my journey. *(CEB)*

Hebrews 4:12

> For the word of God is living and powerful, and sharper than any two-edged sword, piercing even to the division of soul and spirit, and of joints and marrow, and is a discerner of the thoughts and intents of the heart. *(NKJV)*

Psalm 107:20

He sent his word, and healed them,
and delivered them from their destructions. *(NKJV)*
... snatching them from the door of death. *(NLT)*
... he rescued them from the grave. *(NIV)*

He sends forth His word and heals them and rescues them from the pit and destruction. *(AMPC)*

PRAYING THE WORD OF GRACE

Heavenly Father, full of grace, truth and wisdom: Your word is completely pure, and oh, how I love it! Thank You, Father, for the word of grace which You have given through Your Son, Jesus Christ: who is Himself the very Word of God.

Yes, Jesus, You are the Word, who became flesh and dwelt among us here. We beheld the glory of the Father through You, and You are full of grace and truth.

When You walked the earth, Jesus, the people who heard You were amazed at the words of grace You spoke. Yes, they wondered, admired, and were so impressed by the gracious words flowing from Your mouth. They said that no one had ever spoken like You. You spoke with authority, and yet You did nothing on Your own authority, but on the Father's. You spoke just as He taught You. You came in the name of the Father, revealing His glory: a God overflowing with grace and truth.

The words You have spoken are spirit and life. The flesh does not benefit, but it is the Spirit who gives life. You are the Life-giver, Holy Spirit! Your words have given me life!

Oh, how I love Your words! How they fill me with joy! Your beautiful words fill my mind and stir my heart. My heart is welling forth with good things, and overflows with a pleasing theme. I hear Your wonderful word of grace, and my heart responds with love and poetry for my King. My tongue becomes like the pen of a skillful poet.

You are fairer than the children of men, and grace flows from Your lips. Yes, Your lips have been anointed with grace, since God has blessed You forever!

As I discover Your word of grace, I devour every word. Jesus, I listen carefully to Your words, and I feast on them. They are my joy and my heart's delight. Your words fill my heart with bliss. How sweet are Your words to my taste! Yes, sweeter than honey to my mouth. How sweet are Your promises! They have thoroughly tested, and every one proves true. That is why I love them so much!

Your instructions, God, are perfect: renewing my very life. Your words restore and refresh my soul. Your testimony is trustworthy, and makes me wise. Your word discerns the thoughts and intents of my heart. Your word is a lamp before my path, and a light for my journey. It builds me up, strengthens me, and gives me an inheritance.

Your word is alive and powerful, and it heals. Yes, You sent Your word, and healed me. You delivered me from the pit of my destruction. You snatched me from the door of death. You rescued me from the grave. You have called me Your own. Yes, King Jesus, I am named by Your Name.

Father, I pray that in the depths of my innermost being, You would give me ears to hear the word of grace. I pray that You would reveal the wonders of Your truth to me, and let me hear Your words: Your healing, refreshing, edifying, and enlightening words. I open myself to You, so that Your words can pierce through me and do their miraculous work in me. When Your words come, I will listen carefully and feast on them. May the gracious and powerful words of Christ fill my mind and heart. In His precious name, I pray, Amen!

THE LIFE-GIVING POWER OF GRACE-FILLED SPEECH

Colossians 4:6, Ephesians 4:29, Proverbs 22:11, Proverbs 16:24, Ecclesiastes 10:12, Proverbs 15:4, Proverbs 18:21

Colossians 4:6

Let your conversation be always full of grace, seasoned with salt, so that you may know how to answer everyone. *(NIV)*

Let your conversation be gracious and attractive so that you will have the right response for everyone. *(NLT)*

Your speech should always be gracious and sprinkled with insight so that you may know how to respond to every person. *(CEB)*

When you talk, you should always be kind [gracious] and pleasant [winsome; engaging; or wholesome; seasoned with salt] so you will be able to answer everyone in the way you should. *(EXB)*

Ephesians 4:29

Let no unwholesome word come out of your mouth, but if there is any good word for edification according to the need of the moment, say that, so that it will give grace to those who hear. *(NASB)*

Let no corrupting talk come out of your mouths, but only such as is good for building up, as fits the occasion ... *(ESV)* ... but what is good for necessary edification, that it may impart grace to the hearers. *(NKJV)* ... but only such [speech] as is good and beneficial to the spiritual progress of others, as is fitting to the need and the occasion, that it may be a blessing and give grace (God's favor) to those who hear it. *(AMPC)*

... that it may minister grace unto the hearers. *(KJV)* ... Then what you say will do good [give grace; be a gift] to those who listen to you. *(EXB)*

Proverbs 22:11

He who loves purity of heart and has grace on his lips,
The king will be his friend. *(NKJV)*

Whoever loves pure thoughts [hearts] and kind words [lips]
will have even the king as a friend. *(EXB)*

Proverbs 16:24

Gracious words are a honeycomb,
sweet to the soul and healing to the bones. *(NIV)*

Pleasant words are like a honeycomb [liquid honey],
making people happy and healthy ... *(EXB)*
... sweet to the taste and health to the body. *(CSB)*

Ecclesiastes 10:12

The words of the mouth of a wise man are grace: but the lips of a fool shall throw him down headlong. *(DRA)*

The words of a wise man's mouth are gracious and win him favor, but the lips of a fool consume him. *(AMPC)*

Proverbs 15:4

A wholesome tongue is a tree of life,
But perverseness in it breaks the spirit. *(NKJV)*

The tongue that heals is ... *(HCSB)*
A comforting tongue is ... *(BBE)*
Gentle words are ... *(NLT)*

Wholesome speech is a tree of life,
but dishonest talk breaks the spirit. *(CEB)*

A peaceable tongue is a tree of life: but that which is immoderate, shall crush the spirit. *(DRA)* ... but a twisted tongue is a crushing of the spirit. *(BBE)*

A gentle tongue [with its healing power] is a tree of life, but willful contrariness in it breaks down the spirit. *(AMPC)*

As a tree gives fruit, healing words give life [A healthy/healing tongue is a tree of life], but dishonest [deceitful; perverse] words crush the spirit. *(EXB)*

A soothing tongue [speaking words that build up and encourage] is a tree of life, but a perversive tongue [speaking words that overwhelm and depress] crushes the spirit. *(AMP)*

Proverbs 18:21

The tongue has the power of life and death, and those who love it will eat its fruit. *(NIV)*

What you say can mean [In the power of the tongue are] life or death. Those who speak with care [love it] will be rewarded [eat its fruit]. *(EXB)*

PRAYING THE WORD OF GRACE

Heavenly Father, full of goodness, grace and truth, I thank You for Your life-giving word of grace which You have spoken over me. Your word is true and pure, and endures forever. Your word encourages, and brings joy to my heart. Your word washes over me and cleanses me. Your word lights the way to life, and brings light to my eyes. Your word is alive and powerful, sustaining the very world itself. Your word heals, restores, strengthens, and gives life. I cannot thank You enough for Your word!

You have said that the tongue has the power of life and death. You have given me this powerful ability: to actually bring life with my words. How astonishing! I cherish this precious gift, and I thank You that I will be rewarded by the fruit of it. I thank You that you empower me to impart Your grace and favor to those who listen to me. I ask You, Holy Spirit, to teach me to speak with care, that I may speak life-giving words of grace always. May I speak the same life-giving word of grace that You do, God!

May my speech be infused with the Holy Spirit; guided by You. As I follow Your steps and receive Your empowerment, may my words be kind, attractive, pleasant, winsome, engaging, wholesome, and sprinkled with insight. May my conversation always be filled with Your grace, which gives me Your power, along with those who hear me.

And when a direct word is needed for correction, I pray You would anoint my speech with Your grace and sculpt my words with the truth of Heaven's reality. May my words always come from pure truth, love, and life, without any perverseness or speaking words that overwhelm or depress. Thank You, Father, that Your grace always gives me the right response for every person.

Father, I ask that You guide my talk, and I have confidence that You will. May I speak from Your authority and purpose, and not my own, just as Jesus spoke. I ask for Your love, grace and truth to permeate all my heart: so that out of the abundance of my heart, my mouth would speak love, grace and truth!

You are able to make all grace abound toward me, so that always having sufficiency in all things, I may have an abundance for every good work. You are powerfully at work within me, giving me both the desire and the power to do for Your good purposes and pleasure. In Christ, I share in the divine nature of God, and have the fullness of grace! Yes, grace upon grace!

In Christ, who is the Word of Life, my talk is not unwholesome, but I speak good words of grace. My words are fashioned for edification, and they are good and beneficial to the spiritual progress of others, according to the need of the moment. My words are a blessing, a gift, giving grace to those who hear them.

My mouth is a tree of life: my tongue is wholesome, soothing, gentle, and peaceable. When I speak, those around me are built up and encouraged, comforted and healed, and they receive grace and life. My words are gracious and pleasant, and like liquid honey: sweet to the soul and healing to the bones. I speak words of grace that make people truly happy and healthy. When I speak, my words heal and give life!

I love purity of heart, and kind words, and I have Your grace on my lips. I am a wise person, and the words of my mouth are grace, and win me favor. Even the king is my friend, because of Your grace on my lips. The grace in my speech opens doors.

Thank You, Wonderful Father, for speaking Your word of grace over me, which gives me life. In hearing it, I am taught and empowered to freely give what I have freely received. I pray that I may hear Your words of life more and more with an open heart, and that You open my awareness to Your ever-present grace.

I pray that I would fully discover and experience this power of speaking words of life everywhere I go, and that You would reveal to me the greatness of this power that You've given to Your children. May all my speech model Christ Himself, gracious and kind, bold in the truth, filled with love and life. In His name I pray, Amen!

27

DIVINE FAVOR THAT OPENS DOORS FOR GRACE TO MULTIPLY

Psalm 5:12, Psalm 44:3, Genesis 12:2, Revelation 3:7-8, 1 Corinthians 16:9, 2 Corinthians 2:12, Colossians 4:3, Romans 15:15, 2 Corinthians 4:15, Genesis 39:2-4, Genesis 39:21, Daniel 1:9, Luke 2:52

Psalm 5:12

For You, Lord, bless the righteous one;
You surround him with favor like a shield. *(HCSB)*

... You cover them with favor ... *(CEB)* ... you protect them ... *(EXB)*
... as with a shield You will surround him with goodwill (pleasure and favor). *(AMPC)*

... your grace will be round him, and you will be his strength. *(BBE)*

Psalm 44:3

For they did not gain possession of the land by their own sword,
Nor did their own arm save them;
But it was Your right hand, Your arm, and the light of Your countenance,
Because You favored them. *(NKJV)*

For our fathers did not possess the land [of Canaan] by their own sword,
Nor did their own arm save them,
But Your right hand and Your arm and the light of Your presence,
Because You favored and delighted in them. *(AMP)*

... But it was your great power [arm] and strength [right hand].
You were with them [...and the light of your face] because you loved [delighted in] them. *(EXB)*

Genesis 12:2

And I will make of you a great nation, and I will bless you and make your name great, so that you will be a blessing. *(ESV)*

And I will make of you a great nation, and I will bless you [with abundant increase of favors] and make your name famous and distinguished, and you will be a blessing [dispensing good to others]. *(AMPC)* ... [a source of great good to others] *(AMP)*

Revelation 3:7-8

To the angel of the church in Philadelphia write: These are the words of him who is holy and true, who holds the key of David. What he opens no one can shut, and what he shuts no one can open. I know your deeds. See, I have placed before you an open door that no one can shut ... *(NIV)*

... When he opens a door, no one can close it. And when he closes it, no one can open it ... *(EXB)*

... I have opened a door for you that no one can close ... *(NLT)*

1 Corinthians 16:9

There is a wide-open door for a great work here, although many oppose me. *(NLT)*

For a great and important door there is open to me, and there are a number of people against me. *(BBE)*

In spite of the fact that there are many opponents, a big and productive opportunity has opened up for my mission here. *(CEB)*

2 Corinthians 2:12

When I came to Troas to preach the gospel of Christ, the Lord opened a door for me. *(HCSB)*

... a door of opportunity was opened for me in the Lord. *(AMPC)*

Colossians 4:3

At the same time, pray also for us that God may open a door to us for the word, to speak the mystery of Christ, for which I am in chains *(CSB)*

Romans 15:15

But I have written to you very openly [boldly] about some things [points; parts] I wanted you to remember. I did this because God gave me this special gift [or of the grace God gave me] *(EXB)*

But I've written to you in a sort of daring way, partly to remind you of what you already know. I'm writing to you in this way because of the grace that was given to me by God. *(CEB)*

But I have, in some measure, less fear in writing to you to put these things before you again, because of the grace which was given to me by God *(BBE)*

2 Corinthians 4:15

For all things are for your sakes, so that grace, having spread to more and more people, will cause thanksgiving to overflow to the glory of God. *(NASB)*

All of this is for your benefit. And as God's grace reaches more and more people, there will be great thanksgiving, and God will receive more and more glory. *(NLT)*

Genesis 39:2-4

And the LORD was with Joseph, and he was a prosperous man; and he was in the house of his master the Egyptian. And his master saw that the LORD was with him, and that the LORD made all that he did to prosper in his hand. And Joseph found grace in his sight, and he served him: and he made him overseer over his house, and all that he had he put into his hand. *(KJV)*

The Lord was with Joseph [indicating a covenant relationship], and he became a successful man [prospered]. He lived in the house of his master, Potiphar the Egyptian.

Potiphar saw that the Lord was with Joseph and that the Lord made Joseph successful [prosperous] in everything he did. So Potiphar was very happy with Joseph [Joseph found grace/favor in his eyes] and allowed him to be his personal servant [attend him]. He put Joseph in charge of the house, trusting him with everything he owned. *(EXB)*

Genesis 39:21

But the Lord was with Joseph and extended kindness to him. He granted him favor with the prison warden. *(CSB)*

Daniel 1:9

And God gave to Daniel grace and mercy in the sight of the prince of the eunuchs. *(DRA)*

Now God had given the chief of staff both respect and affection for Daniel. *(NLT)*

Now God had established faithful loyalty between Daniel and the chief official; *(CEB)*

Now God made Daniel to find favor, compassion, and loving-kindness with the chief of the eunuchs. *(AMPC)*

God made Ashpenaz, the chief officer [or of the eunuchs], want to be kind [loving] and merciful [gracious] to Daniel, *(EXB)*

Luke 2:52

And Jesus was increasing in wisdom and in years, and in grace before God and men. *(BBE)*

And Jesus kept increasing in wisdom and stature, and in favor with God and people. *(NASB)*

PRAYING THE WORD OF GRACE

Heavenly Father, rich with blessing, I thank You for Your unmerited favor, and for the power of Your grace and Holy Spirit; which all came through Your Son Jesus Christ.

I thank You for placing me in Christ and uniting me with Him! He is the "Righteous One," and has become for me wisdom from God, and my righteousness, holiness and redemption. You made Him who knew no sin to be sin for me, so now, I am the righteousness of God in Him. It is through Him that I enjoy Heaven's complete abundance of favor, blessing, and grace!

Oh Father, Your grace wraps around me! As with a shield, You surround me with Your goodwill, pleasure and favor. You cover me with Your grace. You protect me, and You are my strength. It is not by my strength or power that I save myself, or take hold of my inheritance: it is by Your great power and strength!

I inherit the blessings You have for me, because You love me, You delight in me, and You favor me. I march forward confidently in the strength of Your right hand, and in the light of Your presence; knowing that all of Your promises are "Yes" in Christ. Thank You for Your abundant favor!

Father, I thank You that You bless me in Christ with abundant increase of favors, and You bring greatness and honor through me. You have a powerful purpose for me, and You have blessed me richly so that I will be a blessing; a source of great good to others.

Almighty Father, and Lord Jesus, You hold all the keys. When You open a door, no one can close it. When You close a door, no one can open it. Father, I thank You for the open doors of opportunity You have placed before me, and will place before me, with Your divine favor!

Yes, You open great and important doors for me that no one can close. Regardless of any opposition I meet from any others, Your favor keeps doors wide open for me, for the great work to be accomplished in each mission You have given me. Holy Spirit, I ask You to remind me of this when I face resistance and persecution for doing what You've called me to do. Help me to see the open door!

I pray that You would reveal to me the doors You've opened, and the purposes You've called me to. What are the opportunities that Your favor has opened for me? Holy Spirit, thank You for empowering me to live boldly, daringly, and openly, as I walk through the doors of my destiny.

By the grace You have given to me, may I speak the truth and mysteries of Christ, and live by Your Holy Spirit without fear. As I live out Your purposes for me, and Your grace reaches more and more people, it will benefit everyone I encounter and influence. This will cause thanksgiving to overflow, and You will receive more and more glory!

Father, I thank You also for the discernment to see doors You have closed, that You have not ordained for me to walk through. May I let go of paths You have not designed for me.

Father, I thank You that You cause me to increase in grace before You and before other people. You are able to make my favor multiply, as I grow in wisdom and stature, even as it was with Jesus!

Just as You did with Daniel – as I follow after Jesus and Your Kingdom purposes – I thank You, Father, that You open doors with others whom You want me to influence. By Your grace, may I find grace and mercy in their sight. Give them respect and affection toward me. Cause them to want to give me favor, compassion, and loving-kindness. Establish faithful loyalty and trust. I pray this so that, by Your favor, I may encounter the people You want me to encounter, truly connect with them, and impart Your grace to them through what You've called me to do.

Just as You were with Joseph, I thank You that You are with me in every step of my journey, and You extend Your kindness to me. Father, thank You for granting me favor with those who watch over me. Thank You for Your covenant relationship I have with You, which causes me to prosper and be successful in all I do.

As people see Your hand on my life, and the prosperity You have given me, may I find grace in their sight. As I speak Your word of grace, may Your favor open doors. I thank You now for the doors You open for me to serve others, and the trust and promotions given to me, so that I may influence others with Your love and goodness!

Father, I humbly receive Your grace, which skillfully shapes my heart to be ready for the influence and favor You have prepared for me. Your kindness and goodness lead me to transformation, so may my character be purified, sculpted and filled with Your nature as I encounter Your amazing grace.

Holy Spirit, I welcome You to search my heart and reconstruct my understanding, so I may fully walk as the new person: the grace-filled one You have created and renewed me to be! If there is any way I am not seeing according to Your ways, I ask You to reveal this, and renew my heart and mind. May I have the strength of character that Joseph and Daniel had, and yes, the very character of Jesus Christ Himself! By Your grace, and the power of Your Spirit!

At last, I ask for You to show me how to walk in the fullness of grace and favor, that is mine through Jesus Christ. I ask all of this in His holy name, Amen.

28

GRACE IN DAVID'S PSALMS: THE ANSWER TO OUR PRAYERS

Psalm 6:2, Psalm 31:9, Psalm 57:1, Psalm 143:8, Psalm 36:7-8, Psalm 116:1-2, Psalm 23:1-3

Psalm 6:2

Be gracious to me, Lord, for I am weak;
heal me, Lord, for my bones are shaking. *(CSB)*

Lord, have mercy on [be gracious to] me because I am weak [languish; faint].
Heal me, Lord, because my bones ache [are in agony]. *(EXB)*

Psalm 31:9

Be gracious to me, Lord,
because I am in distress;
my eyes are worn out from angry sorrow—
my whole being as well. *(HCSB)* ...

Be gracious and compassionate to me, O Lord, for I am in trouble;
My eye is clouded and weakened by grief, my soul and my body also. *(AMP)*

... Tears blur my eyes.
My body and soul are withering away. *(NLT)*

Psalm 57:1

Be gracious to me, O God, be gracious and merciful to me,
For my soul finds shelter and safety in You,
And in the shadow of Your wings I will take refuge and be confidently secure
Until destruction passes by. *(AMP)*

... for my soul takes refuge and finds shelter and confidence in You ... *(AMPC)* ...
For my soul trusts in You ... *(NKJV)* ... for the hope of my soul is in you: I will
keep myself safely under the shade of your wings, till these troubles are
past. *(BBE)*

Psalm 143:8

Cause me to hear Your lovingkindness in the morning,
For in You do I trust;
Cause me to know the way in which I should walk,
For I lift up my soul to You. *(NKJV)*

Let me experience
Your faithful love in the morning,
for I trust in You.
Reveal to me the way I should go
because I long for You. *(HCSB)*

Let the morning bring me word of your unfailing love,
for I have put my trust in you.
Show me the way I should go,
for to you I entrust my life. *(NIV)*
... for I give myself to you. *(NLT)*

Psalm 36:7-8

How precious is Your lovingkindness, O God!
Therefore the children of men put their trust under the shadow of Your wings.
They are abundantly satisfied with the fullness of Your house,
And You give them drink from the river of Your pleasures. *(NKJV)*

Your faithful love is priceless, God!
Humanity finds refuge in the shadow of your wings.
They feast on the bounty of your house;
you let them drink from your river of pure joy. *(CEB)*

Psalm 116:1-2

I love the Lord, for he heard my voice;
he heard my cry for mercy.
Because he turned his ear to me,
I will call on him as long as I live. *(NIV)*

I love the Lord because he hears my voice
and my prayer for mercy.
Because he bends down to listen,
I will pray as long as I have breath! *(NLT)*

I love the Lord because he hears
my requests for mercy.
I'll call out to him as long as I live,
because he listens closely to me. *(CEB)*

Psalm 23:1-3

The Lord is my shepherd; I shall not want.
He makes me to lie down in green pastures;
He leads me beside the still waters.
He restores my soul;
He leads me in the paths of righteousness
For His name's sake. *(NKJV)*

The Lord is my shepherd;
I have all that I need.
He lets me rest in green meadows;
he leads me beside peaceful streams.
He renews my strength.
He guides me along right paths,
bringing honor to his name. *(NLT)*

The Lord is my shepherd.
I lack nothing.
He lets me rest in grassy meadows;
he leads me to restful waters;
he keeps me alive.
He guides me in proper paths
for the sake of his good name. *(CEB)*

The Lord is my Shepherd [to feed, guide, and shield me],
I shall not lack.
He makes me lie down in [fresh, tender] green pastures;
He leads me beside the still and restful waters.
He refreshes and restores my life (my self);
He leads me in the paths of righteousness [uprightness and right
standing with Him—not for my earning it, but] for His name's sake.
(AMPC)

Praying the Word of Grace

Faithful Heavenly Father, You are the God who answers prayer! I have
confidence that You have heard me, and will hear me. You answer according to
the abundance of Your grace, through faith in Your Son and His name. In fact,
You have already released every answer for every need, and have provided
complete wholeness through the finished work of Christ. Father, teach me to
trust in this truth revealed in Scripture, and take hold of in prayer what You
have already given in Your grace.

Father, I thank You that You have always overflowed with grace! You revealed
Your grace to Your servant David, the "man after Your own heart," who wrote
about it constantly in his poetry. Your grace is the remedy to my every situa-

tion, and I have received it in abundance, from the fullness of Christ! Grace upon grace!

Because You are full of grace and compassion, I have Your answer for my every need. When I am weak and my bones are aching: I have Your miraculous healing power! When tears blur my eyes, and my soul and body are worn out from anger and sorrow: I have Your restoration, comfort, strength, peace and inner wholeness! When troubles come and destruction seeks me: my soul trusts in You and finds shelter, safety, and confidence under the shade of Your wings! According to Your infinite grace and love, by the precious wounds of Christ: I have full restoration and healing, inside and out, and I have Your secure protection!

Father, I long to take hold of everything You have freely given through the finished work of Your Son. May I truly know and experience the depths of Your love and grace. May I fully experience Your gift of eternal life in knowing You, the one true God. May I walk continually in the Spirit, in the calling for which You have rescued me and called me by Your grace.

Cause me to hear Your loving-kindness in the morning. Let it bring word of Your faithful love. Let me experience Your faithful love, for I have put my trust in You. Cause me to know the way in which I should walk, for to You I entrust my life, and I lift up my soul to You. Father, I give myself completely to You!

How precious, how priceless is Your loving-kindness! Humanity finds refuge in the shadow of Your wings! I am abundantly satisfied with the fullness of Your house, Father, and I will dwell in Your house forever! Thank You, Father, that You give me drink from the river of Your pleasures; Your river of pure joy. My spirit is filled with the ecstasy and bliss of Heaven, through union with Your Holy Spirit! Lead me beside the still waters, and cause me to experience the fullness of this pure joy, restoring my soul!

You my Good Shepherd, Jesus. Because of You, I lack nothing! You feed me, guide me, and shield me, and I have all that I need. You give me rest in the fresh, tender green meadows. You plant me in the field of abundant life and surrounded by the spiritual food of Your grace. You lead me to peaceful streams, beside the restful waters. You keep me alive! You renew my strength. You restore my life, and my whole self is refreshed in Your presence. You guide me along the right and proper paths, bringing honor to Your good name. I have been given uprightness and right standing with You—not due to my earning it, but for the sake of Your name. You have made me whole, and You give me grace upon grace. I am so overjoyed to say that it is You, oh God, who gets all the glory!

Thank You for caring for me with such attentiveness, wise leadership, lavish love, and abundant grace!

I love You, Father. You hear my voice. You have heard my cry for mercy, and You have been so merciful and kind. I have proof of Your unconditional love at the Cross of Christ. I called, and You answered. You turn Your ear to me. You listen closely to me, like a Father bending down to hear His child intently. You intimately connect with me, and You care for me with an everlasting love. Because You are the one who always listens closely: I will pray to You and call on You as long as I have breath. I cast my cares on You, Father, for You care for me.

Thank You for always hearing me. I pray You reveal to me what David saw, and what has been fully manifested through Christ: that You are a God who answers my cry according to Your grace and loving-kindness. You are the Good Shepherd who supplies all my need according to Your riches in glory in Christ.

Reveal to me where You have answered me. And in the places I have not yet seen a breakthrough: show me where You are already on the move. Open my eyes to Your presence and power! Stir up my faith in all You've already given! Increase my wisdom and knowledge of You, and my understanding of the truth of the Good News. Cause me to rest in the meadows of Your grace, by the river of Your life and joy!

I am seen and heard, known and loved by You! How breathtaking. And You have grace for every need, and for every dream You have put in my heart. How unsearchable are Your riches! Thank You, Father, for Your Son Jesus Christ, who is living in me, and is the hope of glory: the glory You have shared with us forever! In His powerful name, I pray, Amen!

29

SURROUNDED BY THE BEAUTY OF GRACE AND GOODNESS

Psalm 23:6, Psalm 90:17, Psalm 33:5, 1 Chronicles 16:34, Psalm 108:4, Psalm 139:7-8, Psalm 16:11

Psalm 23:6

Surely goodness and mercy shall follow me
all the days of my life;
And I will dwell in the house of the Lord
Forever. *(NKJV)*

Only goodness and faithful love will pursue me all the days of my life ... *(HCSB)*

... and through the length of my days the house of the Lord [and His presence] shall be my dwelling place. *(AMPC)*

Psalm 90:17

May the favor of the Lord our God rest on us;
establish the work of our hands for us—
yes, establish the work of our hands. *(NIV)*

And let the [gracious] favor of the Lord our God be on us ... *(AMP)* And let the beauty and delightfulness and favor of the Lord our God be upon us; confirm and establish the work of our hands ... *(AMPC)*

Let the pleasure of the Lord our God be on us: O Lord, give strength to the work of our hands. *(BBE)* ... Yes, make our efforts successful! *(NLT)* ... yes, give us success in what we do ... *(EXB)* ... Make the work of our hands last! *(CEB)*

Psalm 33:5

He loves righteousness and justice;
The earth is full of the goodness of the Lord. *(NKJV)*

He loves whatever is just and good;
the unfailing love of the Lord fills the earth. *(NLT)*

His delight is in righteousness and wisdom; the earth is full of the mercy of the Lord. *(BBE)* ... The earth is full of the lovingkindness of the Lord. *(AMP)*

1 Chronicles 16:34

Oh, give thanks to the Lord, for He is good!
For His mercy endures forever. *(NKJV)*

... For His faithfulness is everlasting. *(NASB)* ... for his mercy is unchanging for ever. *(BBE)* ... His love [steadfast love; lovingkindness] continues [endures] forever. *(EXB)*

Psalm 108:4

For your unfailing love is higher than the heavens.
Your faithfulness reaches to the clouds. *(NLT)*

For Your mercy and loving-kindness are great and high as the heavens! Your truth and faithfulness reach to the skies! *(AMPC)*

Psalm 139:7-10

Where could I go to get away from your spirit?
Where could I go to escape your presence?
If I went up to heaven, you would be there.
If I went down to the grave, you would be there too!
If I could fly on the wings of dawn,
stopping to rest only on the far side of the ocean—
even there your hand would guide me;
even there your strong hand would hold me tight! *(CEB)*

Where can I go to get away from your Spirit?
Where can I run [flee] from you?
If I go [climb] up to the heavens, you are there.
If I lie down [spread out; make my bed] in the grave [Sheol; the grave or the underworld], you are there ... *(EXB)*

... If I go up to the heavens, you are there;
if I make my bed in the depths, you are there.
If I take the wings of the morning,
and go to the farthest parts of the sea;
Even there will I be guided by your hand,
and your right hand will keep me. *(BBE)*

Psalm 16:11

You make known to me the path of life.
In your presence is fullness of joy.
In your right hand there are pleasures forevermore. *(NHEB)*

You reveal the path of life to me;
in Your presence is abundant joy;
in Your right hand are eternal pleasures. *(HCSB)*

You teach me the way of life.
In your presence is total celebration.
Beautiful things are always in your right hand. *(CEB)*

PRAYING THE WORD OF GRACE

Marvelous Heavenly Father! I pour out my gratitude to You, Father, for You are good, and You are gracious! Your mercy is unchanging: it endures forever! Your faithfulness is everlasting! Your steadfast love continues into eternity!

Your mercy and unfailing love are higher than the Heavens. Your truth and faithfulness reach to the skies. The earth is full of Your goodness and loving-kindness. Your delight is in righteousness, wisdom, and whatever is just and good; and Your grace and mercy fill the earth.

Everywhere I look, Your beautiful presence surrounds me. Surely Your goodness and mercy will follow me all the days of my life. I am pursued only by Your grace and faithful love. And through the length of my days, Your house and Your presence shall be my dwelling place. What unfathomable glory!

Where could I go to get away from Your Spirit? Where could I go to escape Your presence? If I climb up to the Heavens, You are there. If I make my bed in the grave, You are there. If I could fly on the wings of the morning, and go to the farthest parts of the sea, even there Your hand would guide me. Even there, Your strong right hand would keep me, and hold me tight. Your presence is everywhere I turn, God; brimming with Your goodness, grace, mercy, and faithful love.

In Your presence is fullness of joy, and total celebration! In Your right hand there are eternal pleasures forevermore. Beautiful things are always in Your right hand, which keeps me and holds me tight. All these things pour out upon me and within me richly!

You make known to me the path of life. I receive Your word, Father, so I may know the way to life. The way and the truth and the life: is Jesus Himself. Thank You for revealing Christ to me. I walk in You, Jesus, and in the Spirit: surrendering to Your presence all around me and within me. Have Your way!

May the gracious favor of the Lord my God rest upon me! Let Your beauty, delightfulness and pleasure rest upon me. Establish the works of my hands for me. Yes, confirm and give strength to the work of my hands. Father, I thank You that by Your abundant grace and favor, You give me success in what I do. You make my efforts prosperous, and You make the work of my hands last.

Father, I am completely surrounded by Your beauty. Your grace and goodness are all around me. Your presence is forever my dwelling place, wherein there is the fullness of Your joy, love, peace, and grace. I am filled with the Holy Spirit, and wherever the Spirit is, there is freedom. Freedom dwells richly within me! I ask that You reveal Yourself in me more and more, so I may fully live in Your infinite grace. In the name of Christ I pray, Amen!

30

GOD'S NATURE: FLOWING WITH GRACE AND FAITHFUL LOVE

1 Timothy 1:14, Psalm 130:7-8, Exodus 33:18-19, Exodus 34:6, Psalm 57:10, Ephesians 1:4-6

1 Timothy 1:14

And the grace of our Lord overflowed, along with the faith and love that are in Christ Jesus. *(HCSB)*

Our Lord's favor poured all over me ... *(CEB)* and the grace of our Lord was more than abundant, with the faith and love which are found in Christ Jesus. *(NASB)*

Psalm 130:7-8

Israel, put your hope in the Lord.
For there is faithful love with the Lord,
and with Him is redemption in abundance.
And He will redeem Israel
from all its sins. *(HCSB)*

O Israel, hope in the Lord;
for with the Lord there is unfailing love.
His redemption overflows.
He himself will redeem Israel
from every kind of sin. *(NLT)*

... For with the Lord there is mercy and loving-kindness, and with Him is plen-
teous redemption ... *(AMPC)* ... for with the Lord is mercy and full salvation.
And he will make Israel free from all his sins. *(BBE)*

Exodus 33:18-19

Then Moses said, "Please, show me Your glory!" And He said, "I Myself will
make all My goodness pass before you, and will proclaim the name of the
LORD before you; and I will be gracious to whom I will be gracious, and will
show compassion to whom I will show compassion." *(NASB)*

Moses responded, "Then show me your glorious presence." The LORD replied,
"I will make all my goodness pass before you, and I will call out my name,
Yahweh, before you. For I will show mercy to anyone I choose, and I will show
compassion to anyone I choose." *(NLT)*

Exodus 34:6

And the Lord passed before him and proclaimed, "The Lord, the Lord God,
merciful and gracious, longsuffering, and abounding in goodness and truth ..."
(NKJV)

Then the Lord passed in front of him and proclaimed: Yahweh—Yahweh is a
compassionate and gracious God, slow to anger and rich in faithful love and
truth *(HCSB)*

Psalm 57:10

For Your faithful love is as high as the heavens;
Your faithfulness reaches the clouds. *(HCSB)*

For Your goodness is great to the heavens ... *(NASB)*
For great is your love, reaching to the heavens ... *(NIV)*

For your great loving kindness reaches to the heavens,
and your truth to the skies. *(WEB)*

Ephesians 1:4-6

For he chose us in him, before the foundation of the world, to be holy and blameless in love before him. He predestined us to be adopted as sons through Jesus Christ for himself, according to the good pleasure of his will, to the praise of his glorious grace that he lavished on us in the Beloved One. *(CSB)*

Even before he made the world, God loved us and chose us in Christ to be holy and without fault in his eyes. God decided in advance to adopt us into his own family by bringing us to himself through Jesus Christ. This is what he wanted to do, and it gave him great pleasure. So we praise God for the glorious grace he has poured out on us who belong to his dear Son. *(NLT)*

[in His love] He chose us in Christ [actually selected us for Himself as His own] before the foundation of the world, so that we would be holy [that is, consecrated, set apart for Him, purpose-driven] and blameless in His sight. In love He predestined and lovingly planned for us to be adopted to Himself as [His own] children through Jesus Christ, in accordance with the kind intention and good pleasure of His will— to the praise of His glorious grace and favor, which He so freely bestowed on us in the Beloved [His Son, Jesus Christ]. *(AMP)*

PRAYING THE WORD OF GRACE

Kind and Compassionate Heavenly Father, Your grace is more than abundant, and it has overflowed to me. Your favor has poured out for me, along with the faith and love that are in Christ Jesus.

Father, thank You, Your redemption overflows. You redeem me from all my sins; every kind of sin. With You there is abundant mercy and loving-kindness, and there is full salvation. I am overwhelmed by Your goodness all around me!

When Moses asked to see Your glory, Your manifest presence, Your very essence: You told him You would cause all Your goodness to pass in front of him. You declared Your name to him, and showed him the truth of Your nature: which is Your goodness! Yes, I see it and declare it: Your glory, and Your very essence is goodness, Father!

You show compassion, mercy and grace to whomever You choose. And Father, thank You that You chose me in the Beloved before time began; to be adopted as Your child, according to the riches of Your glorious grace. You lovingly planned to give me grace, before the beginning of the world and time itself! You are such a Good Father!

I proclaim back to You, Your glory which You proclaimed to Moses: You are a compassionate and gracious God, slow to anger and rich in faithful love, goodness and truth! I worship You, my God, and God of Israel!

Because of Your immeasurable love, You graciously gave Your only Son for my salvation. According to the riches of Your grace, I have been rescued. I will not perish, but have everlasting life. The entire weight of our sin was taken onto the Cross of Jesus, and by His stripes, I was healed. Thank You, Father, for Your immeasurable gift!

This was all according to Your inexhaustible grace and love. Father, Your faithful love and mercy are so great, reaching to the heavens! Your goodness, truth, and faithfulness reach to the clouds!

You have fully revealed Yourself, Father, through Your Son, Jesus. He is Your visible image and very essence, on full display. Through Him, we behold Your glory, and see that You are full of grace and truth. Oh, the glory of Your presence, God!

In Christ, You chose me, even before You made the world. In Your abundant love, You actually selected me for Yourself as Your own. By Your grace, You called me to a holy calling: to be consecrated, set apart for You, purpose-driven, and blameless in Your sight. In Your Son, You have washed me and made me whole!

In Your love, You decided in advance to bring me into Your own family by bringing me to Yourself through Your Beloved Son, Jesus. This was what You wanted to do, in accordance with Your kind intention and good pleasure of Your will: it gave You great happiness. You've always wanted to wrap me in

Your Father's embrace: unhindered, unashamed, untainted, and unafraid. Oh, the bliss of being forever Yours, Abba, Father!

I praise You for the glorious grace and favor, which You have so freely lavished on me in Your Son, Jesus Christ, the Beloved One! It is in His wonderful name I pray, Amen!

31

GOD'S DREAM FULFILLED: EVER LONGING TO GIVE US GRACE

Isaiah 30:18, Numbers 6:24-26,
Psalm 103:4, Psalm 23:5, Jeremiah 31:3,
2 Timothy 1:9-10, Hebrews 13:8-9, 2 Corinthians 6:2

Isaiah 30:18

Yet the Lord longs to be gracious to you;
therefore he will rise up to show you compassion.
For the Lord is a God of justice.
Blessed are all who wait for him! *(NIV)*

For this cause the Lord will be waiting, so that he may be kind to you; and he will be lifted up, so that he may have mercy on you; for the Lord is a God of righteousness: there is a blessing on all whose hope is in him. *(BBE)*

... the Lord waits [expectantly] and longs to be gracious to you,
And therefore He waits on high to have compassion on you.
For the Lord is a God of justice;
Blessed (happy, fortunate) are all those who long for Him [since He will never fail them]. *(AMP)*

... the Lord [earnestly] waits [expecting, looking, and longing] to be gracious to you; and therefore He lifts Himself up, that He may have mercy on you and show loving-kindness to you. For the Lord is a God of justice. Blessed (happy, fortunate, to be envied) are all those who [earnestly] wait for Him, who expect and look and long for Him [for His victory, His favor, His love, His peace, His joy, and His matchless, unbroken companionship]! *(AMPC)*

The Lord wants [is waiting] to show his mercy [be gracious] to you.
He wants to rise and [or is exalted and wants to] comfort [show compassion to] you.
The Lord is a fair [just] God,
and everyone who waits for his help [him] will be happy [blessed]. *(EXB)*

Numbers 6:24-26

The Lord bless you and keep you;
the Lord make his face to shine upon you and be gracious to you;
the Lord lift up his countenance upon you and give you peace. *(ESV)*

The Lord bless you, and keep you [protect you, sustain you, and guard you];
The Lord make His face shine upon you [with favor], and be gracious to you [surrounding you with lovingkindness];
The Lord lift up His countenance (face) upon you [with divine approval], and give you peace [a tranquil heart and life]. *(AMP)*

May the Lord send his blessing on you and keep you:
May the light of the Lord's face be shining on you in grace:
May the Lord's approval be resting on you and may he give you peace. *(BBE)*

... May the Lord smile on you and be gracious to you. *(NLT)*

Psalm 103:4

He redeems me from death
and crowns me with love and tender mercies. *(NLT)*

He keeps back your life from destruction,
crowning you with mercy and grace. *(BBE)*

Who redeems your life from the pit and corruption,
Who beautifies, dignifies, and crowns you with loving-kindness and tender mercy *(AMPC)*

Psalm 23:5

You prepare a feast for me
in the presence of my enemies.
You honor me by anointing my head with oil.
My cup overflows with blessings. *(NLT)*

You prepare a table before me in the presence of my enemies.
You have anointed and refreshed my head with oil;
My cup overflows. *(AMP)*

Jeremiah 31:3

The Lord has appeared of old to me, saying:
"Yes, I have loved you with an everlasting love;
Therefore with lovingkindness I have drawn you." *(NKJV)*

I have loved you with a love that lasts forever.
And so with unfailing love,
I have drawn you to myself. *(CEB)*

... That is why I have continued
showing you kindness [loyalty]. *(EXB)*
... and continued My faithfulness to you. *(AMP)*

2 Timothy 1:9-10

This grace was given us in Christ Jesus before the beginning of time, but it has now been revealed through the appearing of our Savior, Christ Jesus ... *(NIV)*

... that was his plan from before the beginning of time—to show us his grace through Christ Jesus. And now he has made all of this plain to us by the appearing of Christ Jesus, our Savior. *(NLT)*

Hebrews 13:8-9

Jesus Christ is the same yesterday, today, and forever. So do not be attracted by strange, new ideas. Your strength comes from God's grace ... *(NLT)*

2 Corinthians 6:2

For he says,
"In the time of my favor I heard you,
and in the day of salvation I helped you."
I tell you, now is the time of God's favor, now is the day of salvation. *(NIV)*

"At the acceptable time (the time of grace) I listened to you,
And I helped you on the day of salvation."
Behold, now is "the acceptable time," ... *(AMP)*

... Look, now is the right time! Look, now is the day of salvation! *(CEB)*
... Behold, now is truly the time for a gracious welcome and acceptance [of you from God]; behold, now is the day of salvation! *(AMPC)*

... Today is the day of salvation. *(NLT)*

Praying the Word of Grace

Gracious Heavenly Father, I thank You for Your heart, which has been filled with compassion forever. You have loved me with an everlasting love! With Your unfailing loving-kindness, You have drawn me to Yourself. You have continued to show me kindness and loyalty, and have perpetually kept Your faithfulness to me!

Eternally, this is who You are, God: You are Perfect Love!

How wonderful Your heart is, Father. I thank You for Your gracious intention which You've always had within You. You long to be gracious to us! You earnestly wait, looking and expecting, even longing to be kind to me. You rise up to comfort me, and show me compassion and mercy. This is Your nature. This is Your desire.

And I thank You that You are forever a God of justice, and You have justified me freely through the redemption that is in Christ Jesus! I exalt You with whole-hearted joy, Heavenly Father!

I place all my hope in You, Father, and I allow Your abundant blessing to shower down on me! I earnestly long for You; and I am blessed, happy and fortunate, for You will never fail me. Because You are faithful, I confidently expect Your favor, and wait for Your help. With assurance, I am always on the lookout for Your victory in all things.

I open my arms wide to receive Your love, Your peace, and Your joy! Father, I step into the flow of Your matchless, unbroken companionship, freely extended to me already by Your grace. I respond with simple faith by saying "Yes!" I receive Your good, perfect and gracious gifts. Father, I receive You!

How amazing Your grace is, Father. By Your grace, You have redeemed me from death. You have kept back my life from destruction. You have redeemed my life from the pit. I have been saved by Your grace, and this is what You always wanted!

Yes, Father, You crown me with Your grace! You adorn me with Your love! You beautify me and dignify me with Your kindness and tender mercies. You prepare a feast for me, even in front of my enemies. You have honored me by anointing my head with oil. You have refreshed my mind and my whole being by Your grace and Your Holy Spirit. My cup overflows with blessings!

All of this flows from who You are, Lord! This is Your great desire! Thank You, Father, for You have blessed me with every spiritual blessing in the Heavenly places in Christ. I cannot contain my gratitude!

I rest secure in Your embrace, for You bless me and keep me. You protect me, You sustain me, and You guard me. I open myself, and warmly welcome the light of Your face, ever beaming on me graciously. I thank You that You make Your face shine upon me with Your favor. You surround me with loving-kind-ness. You lift up Your countenance upon me, and Your divine approval rests on me. Father, I thank You, that You give me Your peace: a tranquil heart and life to the full.

May my eyes be opened to fully behold You, Father: ever smiling on me, ever gracious to me!

This was Your plan from before the beginning of time, to show me Your grace through Christ Jesus. Yes, Your grace was given to me before the beginning of time. And now it has been revealed through the appearing of Christ Jesus, our Savior. In Him, Your good purposes have been accomplished, and this has brought You great happiness.

Precious Lord Jesus, You are the same yesterday, today, and forever. This has always been who You are, and it has always been Your perfect plan. Sanctify me in the truth of Your word, Father. Keep me from being attracted by any strange, new ideas. I have been entrusted to You and the pure word of Your grace. My strength comes from Your grace. And as I continue to know You more, and place my faith in You, I will continue to grow in this grace in which I securely stand.

You spoke prophetically in ages past, "In the time of my favor I heard you, and in the day of salvation I helped you." I thank You, Father, that according to Your word, the time has come. Now is the time of Your favor. Now is the time of grace. Now is truly the time of Your gracious welcome. I surrender, Father, and fall back into Your arms, receiving Your acceptance of me in the Beloved!

You have listened to me, Father, and You have helped me. In Christ, all things have been made new. Awaken my heart, Father, to the new life and grace You have given to me in Christ. May my heart be filled and flooded with light by the Holy Spirit. May I know and experience the magnitude of Your love.

I come running into Your arms, boldly and fearlessly, as Your dearly loved child, Abba Father! I reach out my hands in awe and gratitude, to freely and openly receive from Your fullness: grace upon grace!

The time for freedom is now. Today is the day of salvation.

In the name of Jesus Christ, I pray, Amen!

EPILOGUE: GRACE IS …

What a beautiful time this has been.

You know, I said at the beginning of this book that I wouldn't attempt a precise definition of grace. So I won't.

Still … It is exciting to look at different ways people have tried to describe it.

In preparing this book, I had such a wonderful time searching out visions of grace. I read words that filled my heart with joy and my face with a smile.

I gathered quotes and ideas from a variety of places like a treasure hunter, from concordances to catechisms … from hymns to theology books … from early church fathers to contemporary writers … describing what grace is, what it does, what it gives, what it's like …

… and at some point I figured out I was compiling a whole other book! Surprise, surprise. Oh well. Maybe I will write that one someday.

My main purpose in this book was really for us to prayerfully immerse ourselves in Scripture, and listen for the glorious theme of grace.

Well, I will say this. As I was searching, I found that the term "grace" seems to cover a lot of ground. Precious, hallowed ground.

Perhaps grace means more than we will ever fully grasp? The original witnesses to the grace of Jesus Christ indicate in the Scripture that Christ's riches are "unsearchable" (Ephesians 3:8, KJV), God's gift is "unspeakable" (2 Corinthians 9:15, KJV), and the riches of His grace are "immeasurable" (Ephesians 2:7, ESV).

That being said, among many glimpses into glory, I did come across this compelling "variation on the theme" of grace in my search.

I began to see this beautiful convergence of different voices from all over the body of Christ through the centuries. This seemed to "reach beyond" typical definitions of grace I was used to hearing.

As they slowly turned the diamond of the gospel of grace in the light of God, they came to behold similar glory … they came to hear a similar variation on the theme …

They came to see that grace is far more than some measured substance or commodity given out by God … and it is beyond simply a kind disposition God has toward us …

Grace is found in the collision of Heaven and earth. It's found in what God does in us and through us. God working within our whole person. This influence is divine, miraculous, complete, eternal. It transforms our being and our doing.

Grace is the place of our participation in the life of God. Where God's very life is in us, and we are in the very life of God. Grace brings us into full communion with the Father, Son, and Holy Spirit.

We experience the sun by its light and warmth. We experience God by His grace. And even greater than the sun, God is eternal, everywhere, all at once.

What a captivating variation on this theme. Grace is the working of God. Grace gives life. Grace transforms. It is the empowering presence that enables us to share in the life of Christ: to partake in Him, and to know Him.

Grace is the gift of God Himself.

How many glorious sides of grace we have witnessed in this book. And yet, however one defines grace … Perhaps, the central purpose of grace is this: to bring us into communion with God, that we may know Him, and share in His life.

Now the whole offer which Christianity makes is this: that we can, if we let God have His way, come to share in the life of Christ ... The whole purpose of becoming a Christian is simply nothing else.

— C. S. Lewis (1898—1963) [1]

To share in the life of Christ. To partake of His divine nature. To join the music, and the dance. To truly know God. To live fully alive in Christ, and be everything we were created for: *with* and *through* and *in Him*. This is our purpose. *This is the purpose of grace.*

By His grace ... we are written into the symphony. We are a sparkle in the diamond. We are the light of the world. *We are a part of it.* We are part of the music and the dance.

Just one more turn of the diamond, friend. I think it will be worth it.

As we behold the glory of God in the eyes of Jesus – the Incarnate Deity, full of grace and truth – *we see Grace personified.*

In his book, *Autobiography of a Person in the Spirit,* Chinese Christian preacher and hymnist, Witness Lee (1905—1997) writes:

Many Christians consider that grace is unmerited favor, something given to us by the Lord freely. I have no objection to this. For instance, Christ's dying on the cross for our sins was something done for us freely. Undoubtedly, this was really grace. Forgiveness and justification are things given by God to us which are of grace. But we must see that the New Testament shows us that grace is nothing less than Christ Himself (1 Cor. 15:10; cf. Gal. 2:20-21) as the very embodiment of the processed Triune God for our enjoyment. Christ has come not merely to do something for us objectively, not merely to bring some good things from God to us freely. The purpose of the work of Christ was so that He could come into us. His dying on the cross was not the purpose but the means to fulfill the purpose of Him coming into us for our enjoyment in order that we may enjoy Him as our life, our life supply, our strength, and our everything. Grace is Christ coming into us as our full enjoyment. [2]

Grace is Christ coming into us as our full enjoyment.

He is our life, and our life supply. He is our strength. He is our everything.

However one defines grace, we can say that grace is the immeasurable gift freely given by God.

Grace means God gives. Best of all, He gives Himself.

Grace is God, and God is grace.

Let us reflect on some of the most precious gifts we've unveiled in our journey praying through Scripture together …

The gift of Christ in us, the hope of glory, the One who finished the work of redemption on our behalf.

The gift of the Holy Spirit in us, who gives life as the One who raised Christ from the dead, the firstfruits of our inheritance.

The gift of the Father in us, who has poured out within us all of His love and glory, the very same that He has always shared with His Son.

Grace has brought us into eternal life, which is intimately knowing God. Grace has brought us into communion with the Father, Son and Holy Spirit. We have become one. The fullness of God in us, and everything of us in God.

Here we see the unsearchable riches of grace.

God is the greatest gift. And what do you do with a gift?

> Man's chief and highest end is to glorify God, and fully to enjoy Him for ever.
>
> — The Westminster Larger Catechism[3]

Enjoy union and communion. Enjoy the sweet music of amazing grace. Enjoy the dance of the fire and the sparkle, and the brilliance in the light. Enjoy the new creation in the garden of God's rest.

And fully enjoy God, *forever*.

Now, "May the grace of the Lord Jesus Christ, and the love of God, and the fellowship of the Holy Spirit be with you all." (2 Corinthians 13:14, NIV)

Amen.

THANK YOU FOR READING!

Reader, *I have a tiny favor to ask*. If you were blessed in reading this, *would you consider giving it a review?* This is one of the *best ways* you can *help us help others*.

My greatest hope in writing this is that God would use my story, pain, and His grace through it all ... to give you something you need in your life's journey. In this, we see our Judah's light and legacy - and God's redemptive power - *shine*.

If you felt a hug of comfort, a deep breath of peace, or were blessed at all from reading this book ... Your review of it makes a *huge* difference in helping it to reach others like you, so they can experience what you have.

Running our little publishing company from our home is a very *challenging*, but *worthwhile* and *exciting* path! As new, self-published writers, we really do rely on the support of our readers. My wife and I are bursting with more stories, passion, hope and inspiration we want to share with the world.

Your review allows us to keep doing what we love. Plus, we read and value every single review that comes in! Not only that, but the words of readers like you are the main way our books will get seen by others. Someone out there may need breakthrough, and your review puts this book at the top of the list in front of them and helps them decide to give it a try.

It only takes a minute to review, and even 1 or 2 sentences helps tremendously!

Review the Book

Scan the QR code to the right, or visit the website below, to take you right to where you can review *Praying the Word of Grace*.

Thank you for considering, *it means so much*. May God bless you richly!

www.lovebuiltpress.com/praying-review

JONAH PRIOUR

Jonah is an award-winning author, Harvard graduate, husband, father, and simple comfort-food-lovin' country guy, raised in the Texas Hill Country.

He returned home in 2012 and met his wife, Faith, where they started their life together serving at the children's home his father founded. There, he was a pastor and worship leader for 10 years, as well as house parent and mentor to some amazing children. Now he writes and publishes books with his wife in the Hill Country while doing ministry, and raising two beautiful children, Miles and Mercy.

Jonah has loved creating and writing since he was little. He also enjoys time in nature, gardening and landscaping, getting lost playing music for hours, adventuring to new (and old familiar) places with his family, snuggling up to a fun show with his wife, and sitting around a campfire with friends. Also sushi.

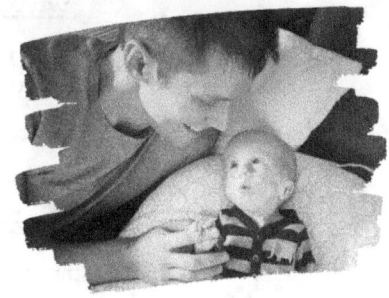

He thinks with a deep smile and welling tears about the day he'll see his firstborn (Judah) again in Heaven. Judah, Miles, Mercy, Faith, and precious Jesus are the sparkle in Jonah's eye as he creates.

Jonah's passion is to create writing, music, experiences and spaces where the Spirit of God moves and sets people free. Free to be fully loved, seen, known, healed, whole, new ... and *fully alive* ... That they may become all they are created to be, and tell the unique story in their hearts.

- a amazon.com/author/jonahpriour
- g goodreads.com/jonahpriour
- BB bookbub.com/authors/jonah-priour

LOVEBUILT PRESS

Lovebuilt Press is a small family-owned publishing house, built with lots of love. We publish inspirational books and content, and we believe that all things done in love have a way of lasting a while, because love never ends. Love remains. So, we put all our hearts into the work we do, praying that God uses it to encounter people with His grace, hope, and perfect love. Our purpose is to set the table for transformation that is real, and inspiration that lasts.

www.lovebuiltpress.com

amazon.com/author/lovebuiltpress

goodreads.com/lovebuiltpress

facebook.com/lovebuiltpress

instagram.com/lovebuiltpress

pinterest.com/lovebuiltpress

FREE STUFF

Want to join our exclusive reader team, and get our stuff for free, before everyone else does?

Our reader team is our core group, our backbone, *the inner circle*. We pray for them, and share how they can pray for us from time to time. We keep them updated when new books, audio or other materials are coming out, and give them free digital copies before the material releases.

Scan here to join our Lovebuilt Reader Team!
www.lovebuiltpress.com/team

TRANSLATION INDEX

AMP — Scripture quotations marked (AMP) are taken from the Amplified® Bible (AMP), Copyright © 2015 by The Lockman Foundation. Used by permission. www.lockman.org.

AMPC — Scripture quotations marked (AMPC) are taken from the Amplified® Bible (AMPC), Copyright © 1954, 1958, 1962, 1964, 1965, 1987 by The Lockman Foundation. Used by permission. www.lockman.org.

ASV — Scripture quotations marked (ASV) are taken from the American Standard Version Bible (Public Domain).

BBE — Scripture quotations marked (BBE) are taken from the 1949/1964 Bible in Basic English (Public Domain).

BSB — Scripture quotations marked (BSB) are taken from The Holy Bible, Berean Study Bible, BSB. Copyright ©2016, 2020 by Bible Hub. Used by permission. All Rights Reserved Worldwide. www.berean.bible.

CEB — Scripture quotations marked (CEB) are taken from the Common English Bible®, CEB® Copyright © 2010, 2011 by Common English Bible.™ Used by permission. All rights reserved worldwide. The "CEB" and "Common English Bible" trademarks are registered in the United States Patent and Trademark Office by Common English Bible. Use of either trademark requires the permission of Common English Bible.

CSB — Scripture quotations marked (CSB) have been taken from the Christian Standard Bible®, Copyright © 2017 by Holman Bible Publishers. Used by permission. Christian Standard Bible® and CSB® are federally registered trademarks of Holman Bible Publishers.

DARBY — Scripture quotations marked (DARBY) are taken from the Darby Translation Bible by John Nelson Darby, 1890 (Public Domain).

DRA — Scripture quotations marked (DRA) are from the Douay-Rheims Bible (Public Domain).

ESV — Scripture quotations marked (ESV) are from The ESV® Bible (The Holy Bible, English Standard Version®), copyright © 2001 by Crossway, a publishing ministry of Good News Publishers. Used by permission. All rights reserved.

EXB — Scripture quotations marked (EXB) are taken from The Expanded Bible. Copyright © 2011 by Thomas Nelson. Used by permission. All rights reserved.

HCSB — Scripture quotations marked (HCSB) are taken from the Holman Christian Standard Bible®, Used by permission HCSB © 1999, 2000, 2002, 2003, 2009 Holman Bible Publishers. Holman Christian Standard Bible®, Holman CSB®, and HCSB® are federally registered trademarks of Holman Bible Publishers.

KJV — Scripture quotations marked (KJV) are taken from the Holy Bible, King James Version (Public Domain).

NASB — Scripture quotations marked (NASB) are taken from the New American Standard Bible®, Copyright © 1960, 1971, 1977, 1995, 2020 by The Lockman Foundation. Used by permission. All rights reserved. www.lockman.org

NHEB — Scripture quotations marked (NHEB) are taken from the New Heart English Bible (Public Domain).

NIV — Scripture quotations marked (NIV) are taken from the Holy Bible, New International Version®, NIV®. Copyright © 1973, 1978, 1984, 2011 by Biblica, Inc.™ Used by permission of Zondervan. All rights reserved worldwide. www.zondervan.com. The "NIV" and "New International Version" are trademarks registered in the United States Patent and Trademark Office by Biblica, Inc.™

NKJV — Scripture quotations marked (NKJV) are taken from the New King James Version®. Copyright © 1982 by Thomas Nelson. Used by permission. All rights reserved.

NLT — Scripture quotations marked (NLT) are taken from the Holy Bible, New Living Translation, copyright © 1996, 2004, 2015 by Tyndale House Foundation. Used by permission of Tyndale House Publishers, Carol Stream, Illinois 60188. All rights reserved.

WEB — Scripture quotations marked (WEB) are taken from the World English Bible (Public Domain).

YLT — Scripture quotations marked (YLT) are taken from the 1898 Young's Literal Translation of the Holy Bible by J.N. Young (Public Domain).

NOTES

3. REMEMBERING THE GOODNESS OF GOD

1. Jenn Johnson, "Goodness of God," track 2 on *Victory*, Bethel Music, 2019, https://open.spotify.com/track/1gj9poFl2mLKkguqWo5Y1i?si=01c2bfe874724f3b.
2. St. Augustine of Hippo, *Confessions*, 1,1.5.

4. WHY GRACE: A MOST GLORIOUS THEME

1. John Newton, "Amazing Grace," 1779.
2. C. S. Lewis Institute, "Amazing Graces: How Complex the Sound!," February 23, 2022, https://www.cslewisinstitute.org/resources/amazing-graces-how-complex-the-sound/.
3. "2 Corinthians 13 (VOICE)," Bible Gateway, n.d., https://www.biblegateway.com/passage/?search=2%20Corinthians%2013&version=VOICE.
4. David Martyn Lloyd-Jones, *Spiritual Depression: Its Causes and Cures* (Zondervan, 2016), 132.
5. John Newton, "Reigning Grace," 1779. (Accessed online: "Reigning Grace.," n.d., https://biblehub.com/library/newton/olney_hymns/hymn_86_reigning_grace.htm.)

7. RECEIVING GRACE BY FAITH

1. Martin Luther and William Russell, *The Ninety-Five Theses and Other Writings* (Penguin Classics, 2017), 27.
2. Charles Spurgeon, *Daily Devotion - 365 Days With Jesus* (Editora Dracaena, 2015), 28.
3. D.W. Martin, *Grace Whisperers: Learning How to Tell the Story of Grace* (Westbow Press, 2020), 58.
4. Martin, *Grace Whisperers*, 63.
5. Martin Luther and Mueller, *Commentary on Romans* (Kregel Publications, 2003), xvii.

8. FAITHFULLY WRESTLING

1. Louisa M. R. Stead (lyrics) and William J. Kirkpatrick (music), "'Tis So Sweet to Trust in Jesus," 1882. (Accessed online: Wikipedia contributors, "'Tis So Sweet to Trust in Jesus," Wikipedia, March 25, 2022, https://en.wikipedia.org/wiki/%27Tis_So_Sweet_to_Trust_in_Jesus.)
2. Martin, *Grace Whisperers*, 65.
3. Stead and Kirkpatrick, "'Tis So Sweet to Trust in Jesus."

9. THE INVITATION: AN ENCOUNTER WITH THE GOD OF GRACE

1. Martin Luther, *Commentary on Galatians* (Zaltbommel, Netherlands: Van Haren Publishing, 2007), 8.

EPILOGUE: GRACE IS …

1. C. S. Lewis, *Mere Christianity* (Touchstone Books, 1996), 153-154.
2. Witness Lee, *An Autobiography Of A Person In Spirit* (Living Stream Ministry, 1994), 83. (Accessed online: "CHRIST AS GRACE," n.d., https://www.ministrysamples.org/excerpts/ CHRIST-AS-GRACE.HTML.)
3. *Larger Catechism Agreed Upon by the Assembly of Divines at Westminster.* United States: Hogan, 1814.